Public Personnel Administration in the United States

Second Edition

N. Joseph Cayer
Arizona State University

Public Personnel Administration in the United States

Second Edition

St. Martin's Press   New York

Library of Congress Catalog Card Number: 85-61242
Copyright © 1986 by St. Martin's Press, Inc.
All Rights Reserved.
Manufactured in the United States of America.
09876
fedcba
For information, write:
St. Martin's Press, Inc.
175 Fifth Avenue
New York, NY 10010

Cover sculpture: from *The City* by Jimmy Grashow.
Cover photo: Stephen Ogilvy.

ISBN: 0-312-65521-5

Contents

6. RIGHTS AND DUTIES OF PUBLIC EMPLOYEES   116

7. LABOR-MANAGEMENT RELATIONS   133

Preface

Since the first edition of *Public Personnel Administration in the United States* was published in 1975, many changes have occurred in the field. Personnel reform at the national level resulted from President Jimmy Carter's attempt to make the federal bureaucracy more responsive. At the same time, state and local governments instituted extensive reorganizations of their personnel management functions. Reflecting the changing political value system, public personnel administrators encountered new concerns. Collective bargaining in the public sector grew at a phenomenal rate during the late 1970s and early 1980s. As an example of how quickly things can change in the political environment, however, collective bargaining is now facing difficult times. Political values and the political environment shape the practice of public personnel management. This book attempts to capture the essence of the accommodation to political forces.

Cutback management and comparable worth are other issues of importance in contemporary public personnel management. Ten years ago, administrators were assuming continued growth in the public sector. Affirmative action and equal employment opportunity were just gaining footholds in the public sector when the first edition appeared. The late 1970s witnessed very aggressive implementation of those policies, but we now have an administration that is deemphasizing and pursuing actions against affirmative action.

Clearly, public personnel administrators are faced with constantly changing pressures and concerns. This book attempts to present public personnel management in the context of changing times and forces. In so doing, students will come to recognize public personnel management for the dynamic process crucial to effective government that it is.

The second edition of this book has benefited greatly from comments and suggestions of many people who read the first edition. Students who have written me and faculty colleagues who have offered ideas are too numerous to mention individually. However, I am indebted to all who have taken the time to suggest ways of improving the manuscript. My own students at the University of Maine, Texas Tech University, and Arizona State University have been very important sources of new ideas and new ways of looking at issues. To them, my sincere thanks for making public personnel management a continually vibrant topic for me.

There are a few people who must be mentioned by name because they have spent much time in helping me with the manuscript. Sherry S. Dickerson and Ned Parrish spent much time in the library searching out items and were also sounding boards for many ideas. Elaine Johansen, University of Connecticut, and William Timmins, Brigham Young University, reviewed the manuscript and offered many suggestions that strengthened the book. To all, my heartfelt thanks.

The staff at St. Martin's Press is extraordinary. It has been a pleasure working with Bob Woodbury, Michael Weber, Peter Dougherty, and Richard Steins. They have shown patience with me when they needed something but have always responded quickly to my needs. I appreciate their good work and professionalism.

Despite the help of so many talented people, there are sure to be shortcomings to this book. For them, I am responsible.

NJC
Mesa, Arizona

Public Personnel Administration in the United States

Second Edition

1

The Environment of Public Personnel Administration

Personnel management encompasses all activities related to people in organizations. It is the utilization of human resources to accomplish the organization's objectives as effectively and efficiently as possible. Because the successful management of people is the key to organizations' effective operation, good personnel management is essential to good administration. In turn, good personnel administration requires both technical and interpersonal skills. Personnel managers must know how to recruit, select, evaluate, promote, train, discipline, and dismiss employees. They must be adept at motivating, counseling, and bargaining with workers. In addition, they are called upon to classify positions, develop compensation plans, measure productivity, and handle grievances and complaints. In short, personnel management involves all aspects of managing the organizations' human resources, and public personnel administration refers to that function in governmental entities.

Personnel administration is also a universal management activity. Every supervisor is, in effect, a personnel manager. Whereas personnel offices normally develop and monitor personnel policies, supervisors are responsible for carrying them out. They are the crucial links in the personnel process, because they deal with employees from day to day. The organization's effectiveness, in turn, hinges in part on how well supervisors perform their personnel functions.

Those who perform personnel activities in the public sector do so in a political environment, and their actions are thus shaped by political considerations. Among these political forces is, first, the competition among interests that have anything to gain or lose from developments within public bureaucracies. Second, the bureaucrats themselves have

1

stakes in the process and so engage in politics to ensure their status. The reactions in 1978 to civil service reform at the national level and more recent attempts to change the retirement system attest to the political involvement of bureaucracies.

Finally, politics includes policy issues that affect and are affected by public personnel administration. Some of these issues are

1. How collective bargaining and merit can coexist.
2. Whether the public service should be used to solve social problems, for example, by being an employer of last resort, taking the lead in affirmative action, or satisfying the demands of myriad special interests who have convincing claims.
3. How to reconcile the continued demands for a higher level of services with the demands for lower taxes and smaller budgets.
4. How to maintain a politically responsive bureaucracy without endangering the concept of merit.

More generally, the public service itself is an issue. The support that presidential candidates such as Jimmy Carter and Ronald Reagan gained for their elections to the presidency by promising to reform the public bureaucracy is one indication of people's concern about government service. Because public policy issues affect the public service, public employees can also influence policy as they help shape and implement it.

In examining the personnel process in government, this book will analyze the specific responsibilities of supervisors and personnel officers and the personnel policies of the process. In particular, it will evaluate the effects that each of the elements has on government's responsiveness and accountability and the ways that alternative approaches affect the delivery of services.

The Field of Public Personnel

Public personnel administration has been accused of not having a sense of identity, being too narrow in scope, and lacking a theoretical foundation.[1] These problems resulted, in large part, from a slavish attachment to principles that seemed appropriate to developing civil service systems to replace the abuses of spoils systems of the nineteenth century. In a zealous effort to remove partisanship from the personnel process, administrators focused almost exclusively on techniques, such as testing and selection methods, that could be applied to personnel activities. Lost in the shuffle was the concern with serving the purposes of management generally. As a result, the rest of management came to perceive personnel administration as a nonpolitical, technical service rather than as management per se. Nineteenth-century reform established a foundation of moral fervor among personnelists that labeled politics as evil and devotion to "neutral" principles of personnel management, as defined by personnelists, as good. As Wallace Sayre noted, public personnel management became "a triumph of technique over purpose."[2] Personnel management lost touch with its environment and became isolated. It assumed a policing role in which it seemed more interested in telling management what it could not do than in finding positive ways to assist it. It is little wonder that the personnel office was regarded with scorn.

But in recent years, personnel students have come to realize that public personnel management is very closely connected with the environment in which it operates. For public personnel administrators, that environment is characterized first and foremost by politics. Whereas the reformers eschewed politics, contemporary personnelists recognize the political nature of their field and criticize the traditionalists for ignoring the relevance of political concerns.[3]

Contemporary observers of public personnel management recognize that the personnel function is driven by the participants' values. These values then affect the types of personnel policies developed, the decision-making rules, and the results of those processes. Conflicts over the values to be represented are resolved through politics,[4] and the error of many personnel reformers has been to equate politics with partisan politics. By focusing on partisan politics, the reformers forgot that decisions were being made by compromising the differing values and interests of those participating in personnel decisions.[5]

There are many different types of public personnel management systems: they may be based on civil service, merit, spoils, or patronage. Civil service systems are characterized by rules and regulations in which personnel activities are insulated from partisan political activity. Merit attempts to differentiate good and poor performance as bases for reward and punishment. Patronage and spoils refer to systems in which those loyal to those in power are rewarded with jobs and opponents are fired or denied employment.

Another way of differentiating personnel systems is according to whether they are management dominated or labor dominated. Historically, public personnel systems have been management dominated, with strict legal limitations placed on the role of labor in the personnel process. Private systems, by contrast, have had a long history of active labor participation. In recent years, of course, management prerogatives in the public sector have given way to bilateral decision making, although there is great variation among governmental jurisdictions.

Today, the civil service and merit concepts prevail in public personnel management. The growth of public sector labor unions, however, has led to many changes in personnel practices. What these changes are and how they affect the personnel process will be examined in Chapter 7. In general, however, the development of unionism in the public sector has sharpened the identification of competing interests in the personnel process. The fortunes of management, employees, elected public officials, citizens, and the bureaucracies themselves all are affected by the changing manner in which personnel is managed.

Although the traditional personnelists exhorted public personnel administrators to apply neutral principles, the presence of competing values makes such an approach impossible. Value judgments must be used in implementing differing employee selection systems, affirmative action programs, and performance evaluation, and all the other elements of personnel systems. Someone will gain and another will lose with each decision made. For example, how is an agency to respond to a cut in its budget? Are the newly hired let go? Are older employees urged to retire early? Are those hired under affirmative action programs protected? Are all departments required to contribute equally to the reduction? Are private vendors used for service delivery? All of these and many other concerns affect the final decision, and each involves a value judgment. Decisions regarding competing value judgments are also political decisions, and so the modern personnel administrator is a participant in the political process.

Public Versus Private Sector Personnel Administration

Public and private sector personnel administration have much in common. For instance, the technical processes used for selecting, interviewing, evaluating, and training employees may be the same in both public and private organizations. But the administration of personnel in the public sector differs from that in the private sector in four important ways:

1. Public employees are subject to more legal restrictions.
2. Lines of authority are less clear in the public sector.
3. Labor-management relations have followed different paths.
4. The political environment affects public personnel to a greater extent.

We shall examine these differences briefly, although the reader should keep in mind that they are blurred by the public and private sectors' interaction and the constant changes in society.

LEGAL RESTRICTIONS

Public employees are usually governed by numerous legal limitations on their activities. Legislation or executive orders require them to refrain from even the appearance of a conflict of interest, that is, the possibility that their official actions will serve their self-interests, economically or otherwise. Personnel administrators and supervisors must monitor their employees' activities as well, to make sure that they have no conflicts of interest, either.

Government employees are often prohibited from engaging in political activities. At the national level, the Hatch Act of 1939 prohibits most partisan political participation by federal employees. State and local governments have their own rules, which sometimes even prohibit participation in nonpartisan elections. These restrictions are aimed at making the delivery of services nonpartisan and to protect employees and citizens from abuses of the spoils system.

After many years of relaxing regulations on personal appearance, dress, and residency, governmental units, especially at the local level, have been reinstituting such rules. For example, police officers may be prohibited from growing beards or long hair, and employees may be required to live in the city in which they are employed. Although employees have challenged such restrictions in the courts, the United States Supreme Court currently has been inclined to side with the employer.[6]

The national government tends to be less concerned with personal behavior as long as it does not affect job performance. Nevertheless, a stricter standard of behavior is generally applied to public employees than to private sector workers. Because citizens pay the taxes that pay government salaries, managers and personnel administrators are sensitive to the image that public employees project, and their concerns have encouraged them to curtail behavior that could create a negative public reaction. When public displeasure is aroused by employees who are intoxicated in public, follow unorthodox life-styles, or promote controversial causes, elected political leaders often put pressure on managers to do something about the "problem." The same pressures are not so likely to appear in the private sector.

LINES OF AUTHORITY

The lines of authority for public employers are much less clear than for those in private enterprise. Although the public agency organization chart may suggest a clear line of authority, it does not show all of the outside pressures brought to bear on public employees' activities. Theoretically, they must respond to the "public interest" and various representatives of the public and interested parties. As David Rosenbloom observed, the constitutional principle of separation of powers fragments political power and creates multiple command points for public employees.[7] Agency employees may be asked to do something different by the chief executive, an influential member of the legislature, a clientele group, and a consumer group. Such multiple command points thus often make it difficult for public employees to decide exactly what they should do in a given situation.

Public employees often face a dilemma regarding which authority should be accorded more attention. Should they respond to their clientele, their superiors, their legislators, or their interpretation of the public interest? The case of Bertrand Berube illustrates this difficulty. He was fired by the General Services Administration (GSA) in 1983 as a result of his publicizing problems of neglect and deterioration in federal buildings in Washington, D.C. His firing ironically came from the same administration that had awarded him a $7500 bonus for similar conduct in 1981, publicizing problems in the GSA under the Carter administration. It therefore is difficult for public employees to know exactly what to do in sensitive situations. What is in the public interest is never completely clear, and each participant in the political process may have a different interpretation. Thus a public employees's action may precipitate a negative reaction from someone in a position to act against the employee. Finally, not only the employee but also the personnel system as a whole must respond to the confusion produced by these multiple commands. Their response normally takes the form of personnel rules and regulations, codes of conduct, and the like. But some of these prescriptions severely limit administrators' flexibility to adapt to differing situations and the organization's differing needs.

LABOR-MANAGEMENT RELATIONS

The public sector has traditionally differed from the private sector, in being almost totally management oriented. There have been exceptions in both sectors: some governments such as those in New York City and Milwaukee, Wisconsin, have had long histories of public sector union activities, and many corporations, especially in the Sun Belt, are fervently antiunion. In general, however, the public sector has only recently begun to share personnel decisions with employees through the bargaining process. The implications for public personnel management have been and will continue to be many, and they will be discussed in Chapter 7.

POLITICAL ENVIRONMENT AND SCRUTINY

Perhaps the most significant factor peculiar to public personnel administration is that the public service is closely watched by the general populace and its representatives. Because the taxpayers foot the bill for government, they are entitled to know what is being done with their money, and in recent years, freedom-of-information acts and open-meeting legislation have become common across the country. With the passage of such legislation, most of the activities of agencies have become subject to public examination, and personnel management must accommodate such scrutiny. Although the personnel decisions themselves are usually exempted from these "sunshine" laws, personnel policies are affected in many ways. The elements of the political environment important to public personnel management include the executive, legislative, and judicial bodies; the media; interest groups; political parties; and the general public.[8]

Executive, Legislative, and Judicial Bodies. The United States Constitution established the separation of executive, legislative, and judicial powers, a model that has also been used in the state and local governments. In theory, public employees are generally under the direction of the executive branch, although employees of the legislature and the judiciary report directly to those branches. In reality, the chief executive has very limited authority over the public bureaucracy. Because most public employees are protected by civil service regulations, the chief executive has little power to change the conditions of their employment or to control their activities. In addition, because the chief executives are usually elected for a fixed and relatively short term, the permanent bureaucracy usually finds it relatively easy to resist direct pressure. Chief executives usually control the appointment of upper-level officials in departments and hope to influence them through that power. However, the number of appointments is usually small in proportion to the total bureaucracy. For example, the president has direct appointment authority for approximately four thousand positions out of a civilian bureaucracy of close to three million. Many of these appointive positions include judges and officers of regulatory agencies who, once appointed, are independent of the president, thus severely limiting the chief executive's ability to direct the bureaucracy through the power of appointment. The legislative body and judiciary limit that authority even more through the legislature's confirmation power and the judiciary's review of attempts to dismiss employees.

Through the budget process, the executive and legislative bodies have great impact on the personnel system. Because the chief executive is responsible in most governments for developing budget recommendations, agencies must be aware of the administration's desires. They work hard to ensure adequate funds for their personnel needs, as a loss of funds normally means a reduction in the number of employees for the agency. Once the chief executive makes the recommendations to the legislative body, the agency's attention turns to legislative politics. There it is often possible to increase agency budgets through mobilization of clientele and good work by the agency personnel, thus demonstrating to the legislative body the agency's needs. Of course, agencies can often get caught up in a struggle between the executive and legislative branches. At the national level, for example, conflicts over the budget routinely lead to federal employees' receiving no paycheck at the end of a fiscal year. Ordinarily, Congress then passes an emergency resolution authorizing the agencies to continue operating until a budget is finally adopted. Nonetheless, it is difficult to plan when the agency does not know whether it will have a budget for the next year.

The basic policy concerning public personnel is generally determined as a result of executive and legislative efforts. The Civil Service Reform Act of 1978 represents a significant change in federal public personnel policy, and state and local governments have used the act as a model for action at their levels. Conflicts between the president and Congress regarding this act were many, and other interested parties pressed to have their concerns addressed. Although the Carter administration pushed the reform as one of its principal programs, Congress made its imprint by modifying and eliminating many of the act's provisions. Each branch played its role in the policymaking process to come up with the final product. Now the Office of Personnel Management, the Merit Systems Protection Board, and the Federal Labor Relations Authority must define the policy through their rules, regulations, and decisions. Additionally, the judicial branch will participate through litigation concerning the act's provisions and agency decisions.

The separation of powers doctrine also affects the personnel system, in that all branches of government have some effect on public employees. The personnel manager and agency manager must be aware of each branch's interests and decisions in order to carry out personnel policies. Missteps by public employees may be exploited by those in political office if it will work to their advantage. As such, the public manager and employee are under much pressure that does not apply to any great extent to the private sector employee.

The Media. It is difficult to imagine a force in the political environment with a greater potential for influencing public personnel administration than the communications media have. Because of the constitutional guarantees of freedom of the press and speech in the United States, the media can keep the public well informed about the public service and its activities and problems. Indeed, the public and political actors depend on the media for much of their information. Even though the press often focuses on the negative aspects of the public service, it is frequently responsible for many improvements. Many problems in the public service are brought to light and scrutinized by the media, whereas the private sector rarely undergoes such close examination of its staff or personnel policies and practices. The media cannot, however, ensure that agency personnel continue to perform effectively. They are unlikely, for example, to expose an unenthusiastic performance of duties (which is an important evaluation of the public service).

Interest Groups. Many interest groups also exert pressure on public personnel operations. Among these are clientele groups, minority and women's groups, public interest groups, professional associations, civic groups, taxpayer associations, and public employee associations and unions. Although interest groups generally are most concerned about issues other than personnel management, they do recognize that having some power over which people make decisions will influence the agency's response to their concerns.

Some groups tend to concentrate on relatively narrow issues of self-interest. Thus, clientele, minority, women's, professional, and public employee groups are likely to seek policies that will make sure that the agency gives their particular welfare as much consideration as possible. Public interest and civic groups such as civil service leagues, good government associations, the League of Women Voters, taxpayer reform associations, and the Center for the Study of Responsive Law take a more general approach. They pursue policies beneficial to the "public interest" and usually promote personnel systems that reduce the potential for partisan political influence. They also tend to favor policies that require public employees to disclose personal financial interests and that control conflict-of-interest situations.

Political Parties. Political parties and politicians have always had an interest in public personnel operations. Politicians often view patronage as a means of exerting control over and ensuring the responsiveness of public employees. Furthermore, politicians often find public bureaucrats easy targets for political rhetoric and so exploit public service problems and inadequacies for political purposes. In fact, we should note that public personnel reform came about partly because politicians did use corruption and inefficiency as issues; therefore, personal political gain may not always be the overriding concern behind such appeals. Too often, however, the criticism of the public service does little to improve it and serves merely to denigrate it.

Certainly, the exploitation of the public service for political demagoguery is not as extensive today as it once was, but many politicians still run their campaigns on a platform that includes references to the "incompetent" or "oversized" public bureaucracy. Indeed, President Ronald Reagan promised to reduce the government's size, a promise whose implications for personnel management are obvious. But virtually every candidate for governor or mayor promises the same thing, and it is not too surprising that those elected then have difficulty with the employees of their governments.

The political parties have traditionally depended on government jobs as a way of building up party strength, but the continued trend toward using comprehensive merit systems has greatly diminished this source of support. Louisiana, Indiana, and New Jersey, however, demonstrate that patronage is alive and well in many state bureaucracies. And local government still indulges in political favoritism, too, as illustrated by the recent experiences of cities such as Chicago, Boston, and Philadelphia. In Louisiana, the governor was indicted as the result of favoritism and in Boston, Mayor Kevin White's tenure ended with many charges of influence peddling among his close aides and appointees.

The General Public. In a democracy, the public service is supposed to serve the interest of the general public. The problem is in defining what the "public interest" is. Responsiveness to the public and its wishes, which are difficult to determine, is one aspect of serving the public. Some prefer to consider that a responsible public service is one that is effective in achieving the system's long-range goals, though this approach sometimes runs counter to the public's wishes.[9] What is important to the administration of public personnel is that the public expects responsiveness, but many political leaders exploit this expectation by promising attractive but impractical solutions to voters' problems. Other individuals and groups, particularly public interest groups, direct their attention to long-range objectives, and public administrators, including personnel administrators, are caught in the middle.

The public's view of bureaucracy is determined by the society's general value system. People's assumptions about the work ethic, self-reliance, and individualism will color their response to the public service, especially as society weighs the effects that government programs and employees have on these values. The common impression is that the public service is composed of indolent, secure employees who have too much power over people's lives and consume tax money with little beneficial effect. These views, along with the idea that the bureaucracy is oversized and uncontrollable, make it difficult for the public service to recruit employees.

It is ironic that the Reagan administration, which came to office in part because of its own denigration of the public service, has contributed to further distrust of the system rather than doing anything to change this perception. The administration's relentless attacks on the public bureaucracy continue to reinforce people's negative perception of it. Even more damaging, however, have been the ethical conflicts in which many high-level appointees have engaged. While preaching the necessity of purifying the career bureaucracy, the top-level appointees have been constantly embroiled in controversies concerning their ethical conduct. Even Edwin Meese, appointed as the Attorney General, the chief law enforcement officer of the United States, had his confirmation held up because of numerous instances and charges of questionable legal and ethical conduct. It is no wonder that the general public has difficulty believing in the public service's integrity. And of course, Congress has not helped, either, with its sex and bribery scandals. At the same time the executive and legislature search for abuse in the public service, they have difficulty keeping their own houses in order.

Summary

Public personnel management resides in a complex environment and is part of a larger governmental system. Because the system in the United States contains a variety of interests competing for position and power, the personnel system becomes entwined in the political process. The various political actors and forces outlined in this chapter obviously have different interests in the personnel system. The personnel function cannot be viewed as a neutral instrument of management; rather, it is at the center of the decison-making process and can easily become a pawn in the struggle for political power and influence. Although all of the actors, such as the president and members of Congress, insist that they want only the most efficient and responsive public service possible, they actually may be primarily concerned with maintaining or improving their political position. Thus, expressions of outrage from either side regarding personnel actions are often calculated more for political advantage than for improving personnel practices. Similarly, other participants in the political environment have conflicting interests, which can lead to compromise and accommodation in public personnel management.

This chapter has identified the role of public personnel management in the governmental process, and it has introduced the major forces that affect public personnel management and the issues that are of concern to personnel managers. The remaining chapters will elaborate on these topics. Chapters 2 and 3 will focus on political considerations in the development of public personnel systems. Chapter 2 will trace the evolution of public personnel management, and Chapter 3 will examine some of the enduring political forces that shape the way that the management of personnel is organized in government. Chapters 4 and 5 will evaluate the technical tools and techniques used by personnel managers, and Chapters 6, 7, and 8 will consider some of the challenges to traditional public personnel management. Finally, Chapter 9 will look at what lies ahead for public personnel administration.

NOTES

1. David H. Rosenbloom, "Public Personnel Administration and Politics: Toward a New Public Personnel Administration," *Midwest Review of Public Administration*, 7 (April 1973), 98–110. For a discussion of the lack of theory, see Donald E. Klinger and John Nalbandian, "Personnel Management by Whose Objectives?" *Public Administration Review*, 38, no. 4 (July-August 1978), 366–372; and H. Brinton Milward, "Politics, Personnel and Public Policy," book review essay, *Public Administration Review*, 38, no. 4 (July-August 1978), 391–396.

2. Wallace S. Sayre, "The Triumph of Technique over Purpose," *Public Administration Review*, 8 (Spring 1948), 134–137.

3. One of the first to recognize the importance of the political environment was Frederick C. Mosher, *Democracy and the Public Service*, 2d. ed. (New York: Oxford University Press, 1982.) A classic in the field is by Frank J. Thompson, *Personnel Policy in the City* (Berkeley and Los Angeles: University of California Press, 1975). Also, Muriel M. Morse, "We've Come a Long Way," *Public Personnel Management*, 5 (July-August 1976), 218–221, does a good job of explaining public personnel management principles and their legacies.

4. Among them, David H. Rosenbloom, "The Sources of Continuing Conflict Between the Constitution and Public Personnel Management," *Review of Public Personnel Administration*, 2 (Fall, 1981), 3–18; Wilbur C. Rich, *The Politics of Urban Policy: Reformers, Politicians and Bureaucrats,* (Port Washington, N.Y.: Kennikat Press, 1982); Chester A. Newland, "Public Personnel Administration: Legalistic Reforms vs. Effectiveness, Efficiency, and Economy," *Public Administration Review*, 36 (September-October 1976), 529–537; and Theodore J. Lowi, "Machine Politics—Old and New," *The Public Interest*, 9 (Fall 1967), 83–92.

5. Thompson, *Personnel Policy in the City* and his "The Politics of Public Personnel Administration," in Steven W. Hays and Richard C. Kearney, eds., *Public Personnel Administration: Problems and Prospects* (Englewood Cliffs, N.J.: Prentice-Hall, 1983), pp. 3–16.

6. *Kelley* v *Johnson*, 425 U.S. 238 (1976), and *McCarthy* v *Philadelphia*, 96 U.S. 1154 (1976).
7. David Rosenbloom, "Public Policy in a Political Environment: A Symposium," *Policy Studies Journal*, 11 (December 1982), 245–254.
8. Bruce Adams, "The Frustrations of Government Service," *Public Administration Review*, 44 (January-February 1984), 5–13.
9. See Francis E. Rourke's excellent discussion of responsiveness and effectiveness in *Bureaucracy, Politics, and Public Policy* (Boston: Little, Brown, 1969), pp. 3–6.

SUGGESTED READINGS

Adams, Bruce. "The Frustrations of Government Service." *Public Administration Review*, 44 (February 1984), 5–13.
Hays, Steven W., and Richard C. Kearney. *Public Personnel Administration: Problems and Prospects.* Englewood Cliffs, N.J.: Prentice-Hall, 1983.
Loverd, Richard A. "Approaching the Management of Public Personnel Administration: A United States Perspective." *International Studies of Management and Organization*, 12 (Fall 1982), 33–42.
Lowi, Theodore J. "Machine Politics—Old and New." *The Public Interest*, 9 (Fall 1967), 83–92.
McGregor, Eugene B., Jr. "The Great Paradox of Democratic Citizenship and Public Personnel Administration." *Public Administration Review*, 44 (March 1984), 126–132.
Mosher, Frederick C. *Democracy and the Public Service,* 2d ed. New York: Oxford University Press, 1982.
Newland, Chester A. "Crucial Issues for Public Personnel Professionals." *Public Personnel Management*, 13 (Spring 1984), 15–46.
Rabin, Jack, Thomas Vocino, W. Bartley Hildreth, and Gerald J. Miller. *Handbook on Public Personnel Administration and Labor Relations.* New York: Marcel Dekker, 1983.
Rich, Wilbur C. *The Politics of Urban Personnel Policy: Reformers, Politicians and Bureaucrats.* Port Washington, N.Y.: Kennikat Press, 1982.
Rosenbloom, David H. "Public Policy in a Political Environment: A Symposium." *Policy Studies Journal*, 11 (December 1982), 245–254.
———. "The Sources of Continuing Conflict Between the Constitution and Public Personnel Management." *Review of Public Personnel Administration*, 2 (Fall 1981), 3–18.
Selznick, Philip. *TVA and the Grass Roots.* Berkeley and Los Angeles: University of California Press, 1949.
Thompson, Frank J., ed. *Classics of Public Personnel Policy.* Oak Park, Ill.: Moore, 1979.
———. *Personnel Policy in the City.* Berkeley and Los Angeles: University of California Press, 1975.

Case 1.1: Dealing with Political Pressure

As you, Hal Conry, return home after a long conference, you look forward to having time to get caught up on work that has been neglected because of the many special projects assigned to your office. As director of the state Department of Health Resources, you realize that the many conflicts over health care services and costs are very much on the minds of citizens and legislators alike. At the moment, the legislature is in the process of considering your agency's budget, and your new health cost containment program is politically controversial, given its many cost overruns in the past. In addition to catching up on your other work, you are scheduled to testify in a couple of days before the legislature's Committee on Health and Human Resources.

On your way to the office, you hear on the radio news that the director of one of your children's care facilities and his wife are in a bitter divorce trial. Ordinarily the divorce would not be newsworthy, but it has come out in the trial that the director, John Shore, was accused by his wife of physical abuse during their marriage. Shore admitted that in the early years of marriage, he had been a physical abuser, but he insisted that he had sought counseling for and had overcome the problem, with the result that he had not been abusive during the past seven years. But because of his high position with the children's center and because of the recent concern with child abuse, the information was a major news feature.

Upon arriving at the office, there were calls waiting for you from the governor, several legislators, and many reporters. You return the governor's call and that of the chairperson of the Committee on Health and Human Resources. The message is the same from both: "Shore is a political embarrassment who must be relieved of his duties." You are in a difficult position because you know Shore to be one of the most effective administrators in your department. You also know that the funding of your agency and perhaps your own position could be in jeopardy. Before you return your other telephone calls, you decide to think through the situation and arrive at a response.

INSTRUCTIONS:

Explain the options you have considered in dealing with this situation. Indicate your reasons for and against using each. What is your final decision, and why?

Case 1.2: Sabina

Sabina Crane is a career counselor at Maybridge High School. She has been with the school district for five years and each year has received outstanding evaluations for her performance, as well as the maximum merit pay increases available to her. She has also been given awards from national organizations for her work with high school students.

To her surprise, Sabina was notified by the superintendent's office that her contract for next year was not being renewed. Because the contracts for her position had been relatively automatic, nonrenewal meant that essentially she had been fired. When she asked the superintendent's office for an explanation, she was told that her personal life-style was not compatible with her work with high school students. Pressing further, she learned that the superintendent's office had been told that she was bisexual and had a female lover. She did not deny this but felt that it had nothing to do with her ability to do her job. As a result, she appealed the decision but was unsuccessful with the appeals board. Finally, she took her appeal to the school board.

INSTRUCTIONS:

The school board is made up of five members, all of whom were elected. Four of the members have made public their reaction to this case, and they are divided evenly, with two supporting the superintendent's office's position and two supporting Crane's request to be renewed. You are the fifth member of the board. How will you vote? Explain. Some information that might help you: The state has no legislation either protecting the right of gays to hold jobs or prohibiting the employment of gays.

2

Evolution of the Personnel System

All governments face the problem of how to staff and maintain a public service that at the same time must be consistent with national political goals, competent, loyal to management, and responsive to the public. There has been constant conflict among these competing criteria for the establishment and operation of a personnel system, and there have been numerous and dramatic changes in the public service as accommodations to ever-changing political, social, and economic realities.

As noted earlier, this book's major premise is that public personnel administration can best be understood in terms of its relationship to political values and processes. Therefore, the brief historical overview of the public service presented in this chapter will emphasize the influence of political values on the public personnel operation. First is the period of early development, 1789 to 1829; the period in which spoils predominated, 1829 to 1883; the period in which the merit system developed and dominated, 1883 to 1978; and finally, the period of contemporary reform, 1978 to the present. During each of these time spans there were significant events that might be used to categorize further the development of public personnel administration, but the periods suggested here break at the times at which major new perspectives on the public service emerged.[1] The last section of this chapter will evaluate the legacies of each period.

The Early Roots

President George Washington is usually credited with developing a competent public service. Because there was, of course, no established bureaucracy when he assumed the presidency, he was in the unique position of being able to build a public service from scratch. Although political considerations are not usually attributed to Washington in his personnel actions, he did in fact make numerous concessions to political reality.[2] He was not so politically partisan, however, as many of his successors were.

One of the realities with which Washington had to contend was that political power in the nation's early years was held almost exclusively by the aristocracy. Although Washington established fitness and ability as requirements for appointment to the public service, fitness usually meant social status or prestige rather than technical competence.[3] Washington was free to use such a definition because the tasks of the public bureaucracy were not highly specialized, as they were later when our social and political systems became more complex. The important point is that Washington chose public servants from the politically powerful sector of society.

Washington was influenced by other political considerations as well. He had the enormous task of integrating a new nation of previously independent-minded units, and to do so he had to plan and act carefully. A significant requirement for public service employment under Washington was support of the new federal political system. Although support for the political system does not seem particularly radical today, it was a controversial issue at the time, as many people hoped the new system of government would fail. Thus, oddly enough, a political position with which many citizens strongly disagreed was a requirement for holding a public job.

There were also regional considerations. President Washington wanted to ensure that local programs would be administered by the members of each community and that all regions of the country would be represented in the high echelons of the public service. He thereby hoped to gain nationwide support for and identification with the new political system.

Still another political move by the new president was to defer to the wishes of Congress on many appointments. Recognizing that members of Congress could greatly affect his administration's success, Washington conferred with them, even though he was not legally required to in most instances. Indeed, presidents still consider congressional wishes in their appointments. Another group accorded special attention by Washington were the Revolutionary army officers. They were often hired in preference to others, although Washington was careful to limit the extent of such appointments. Preferential treatment of veterans, now common in the national as well as state and local merit systems, derives in part from Washington's policies.

That Washington's decisions were often politically motivated should not come as a surprise. In a democratic system it is expected that public officials will respond to political forces. But what is surprising is that until recently, many scholars have described Washington's public personnel policies only as competent and honest, paying little attention to the role played by the political environment. As Van Riper found, it is fortunate that these political considerations were consistent with the development of a highly competent public service,[4] as many of these political accommodations left enduring marks on the staffing of public bureaucracies. Regional representation, partisan political support, loyalty, preference for veterans, and consultation with members of Congress have been and often still are significant concerns in filling public service positions.

George Washington's immediate successors made few changes in his approach to staffing the public service. Partisan concerns became more important under John Adams, but Thomas Jefferson made the most significant break with Washington's practices. Representing a new party in power, Jefferson wanted to reward his Republican followers with appointments. The long years of Federalist control, however, had resulted in the entrenchment of Federalists in public service positions. To obtain a bureaucracy more to his liking, therefore, Jefferson removed many government employees, justifying this policy by claiming a need for balance in partisan viewpoints.[5] He believed that because the people had elected him president, they should have like-minded public servants to help him carry out his policies, a view that all modern presidents also articulate. Political party affiliation was not Jefferson's only criterion; he also insisted on ability and fitness in the way that Washington did. Jefferson was the real father of spoils in the sense of bowing to party pressure in appointments; yet he diligently resisted debasing the public service by making it strictly partisan.

Jefferson's successors followed much the same tradition, just as those succeeding Washington accepted his lead in staffing the public service. Although partisan politics became more important during Jefferson's presidency, the character of the public service remained virtually unchanged. Despite his Republican philosophy, Jefferson still had to contend with the politically powerful elite. Consequently, the aristocracy retained its hold on public service positions through the administration of John Quincy Adams. The tests of loyalty, regional considerations, preference for veterans, and consultation with Congress remained factors in public service staffing.

Jacksonian Democracy

With a dramatic shift in the center of political power came an equally dramatic change in the public bureaucracy. The election of 1828 brought to a head the political frustrations that had been building up in the populace. From 1800 to 1829 the United States political system became more democratic, in that new groups in society gained the opportunity to participate in politics. The addition of eleven states—nine in the West—brought a new flavor to politics and elections. Previously, only landowners and the aristocracy had had the vote, but electoral reforms in the early nineteenth century and the admission of new states in which the common man ruled greatly broadened electoral participation. The western states led in extending the suffrage, but by 1829 the right to vote was almost universally enjoyed by white males. The admission to the union of the western states also changed the power relationship between the upper and lower classes in favor of the lower. And the egalitarianism of the frontier brought its influence to national politics.

The extension of suffrage resulted from political considerations. With more voters, the parties could increase their ranks and thus saw the advantage of extending the right to vote. As the common man participated in the choice of elected political leaders, he also expected some of the fruits of politics, and so it is not surprising that resentment toward the aristocracy's monopoly on public service positions developed. Astute political leaders could not ignore the expectations of their new constituents. Recognizing that political patronage could be used to build up their parties, politicians made the spoils system a standard feature of public service staffing in state and local government.

The triumph of the common man reached the national level with the 1828 election of President Andrew Jackson. His inauguration celebrations are often cited as an example of the dramatic change in the locus of political power. The social critics of the day were aghast at the antics and crudeness of Jackson's followers, many of whom descended upon Washington in search of government employment.[6]

The expectations of Jackson's followers were high, and the genteel elements of Washington politics anticipated disaster. As it turned out, the expectations of both groups were exaggerated. Jackson was interested not only in realigning the public service's political makeup but also in reducing government activity and hence the size of the bureaucracy. Consequently, the hordes of office seekers found that Jackson meant to cut back on government jobs. On the other hand, and most important to our consideration, Jackson followed Jefferson's lead in insisting that the bureaucracy reflect the results of the election, and accordingly he removed many people from office and replaced them with his own followers.

Although Jackson did not turn out a significantly higher proportion of employees from the public service than did Jefferson, he is more closely identified with the spoils system because he was more openly partisan and proud of it. He saw his administration as one that revolutionized the American political system. His administration broke the aristocracy's political power over both elective and appointive positions. The revolutionary character of Jackson's approach was that the public service was democratized in response to the democratization of the electoral system.

The shift in political power caused intense criticism of Jackson's public personnel policies. However, despite his feeling that the government's work was so simple that anyone could do it (much truer then than today), Jackson still insisted on competence and the judicious use of patronage. He would have been as uncomfortable as any of his predecessors to see the extent to which many of his successors used and abused patronage.

Weakening of Spoils

After Jackson's administration, the alternation of political party control of the presidency led to a revolving door for public servants, with the door taking four years to complete a revolution. Even though there were many carry-overs from one administration to another, they were usually assigned to different positions. Even the election of a president of the same party, as when James Buchanan succeeded fellow Democrat Franklin Pierce, did not ensure the retention of the same public servants. Rather, Buchanan represented a different faction of the party and was pressured into changing the bureaucracy to reflect that.

The election of Abraham Lincoln in 1860 represents both the high point and the onset of the demise of the spoils system. Lincoln used the system to a greater extent than any other president had. Mobilizing the Union for the Civil War required a loyal public service, and Lincoln felt that the only way to do this was to use patronage.[7] Lincoln's sweep of people from office, the most extensive in United States history, was warranted by the political considerations of the time. His concern was to consolidate the Republican party, which had been in disarray, and to carry out a major and controversial war. As the Union began to come apart, officeholders from the South were removed, and those loyal to the Union were put in their places.

Despite his wide use of the spoils system, Lincoln must also be credited with initiating its gradual decline. After his election to a second term, he was put under a great deal of pressure to make a clean sweep of his appointees, as his supporters had become accustomed to a completely new team every four years. Lincoln's refusal to oblige thus gave hope to critics of the spoils system and led to an examination of the system that produced significant change in the coming two decades. President Andrew Johnson, faced with internal political problems of his own, found it necessary to replace many of Lincoln's loyalists; but the spoils system was marked for destruction, and in less than twenty years it was dealt a blow from which it never recovered. In the years between Lincoln's administration and 1883, political forces gradually chipped away at the patronage system. Much like the growth of democratic political participation from 1800 to 1829, the growth of discontent with the spoils system from 1865 to 1883 led to a revolution in the staffing of the United States government bureaucracy.

The Civil War greatly increased the power of the executive branch vis-à-vis Congress, and the end of the war brought an opportunity for Congress to attempt to regain some of its influence. With Andrew Johnson in office and with his internal party struggles, the stage was set. The area of greatest struggle, and also the immediate issue in Johnson's impeachment proceedings, was control over government personnel. The difficulties Johnson had with Congress and his party led him to drop many of Lincoln's appointees in favor of his own. Predictably, such action only heightened congressional opposition to him.

The Tenure of Office Act of 1867 symbolized Congress's attempt to gain control over patronage. The act limited the president's removal power to the extent that removal required Senate approval in cases involving officers who had previously been appointed with Senate confirmation. Defiance of Congress and the act led to Johnson's impeachment by the House of Representatives; the Senate acquitted him by only one vote. Appointment and removal power was the immediate issue over which this momentous confrontation developed, but the political issues were much broader. For the student of public personnel, however, it is a significant occasion because it signaled a movement away from presidential control over patronage and personnel policy issues. Congress subsequently consolidated its power over the general policy in the next decade and a half. Eventually, congressional interest led to the establishment of the merit system, although its major interest at this point was controlling spoils.[8]

President Johnson's lack of control and the weak administrations of Ulysses S. Grant and Rutherford B. Hayes produced even greater congressional interest in, and control over, the personnel process. At the same time, efforts for reform were being made. During Grant's administration, Congress passed the Civil Service Act of 1871, although its proponents had to attach it as a rider to an appropriations bill as the only way to get it passed.[9] Suprisingly enough, President Grant was a supporter of civil service reform and had actually proposed legislation similar to that passed in 1871. More importantly, to the surprise of many Republicans in Congress, he tried to institute a merit system. In effect, the act of 1871 reestablished presidential control over the personnel process by giving the president authority to establish rules and regulations for employees in the public service and to appoint advisers to help draw up and administer the rules and regulations. Grant did just that by appointing a seven-member civil service commission and issuing executive orders for the limited use of merit concepts.

But political realities did not permit Grant's experiment with reform to endure. Congress was not willing to give up the control it had. Fearing a loss of power through a loss of patronage, Congress refused to fund the system after 1873, and so it was no longer able to operate, although some commissioners did work without compensation. Despite its short tenure, Grant's commission did have lasting effects: its recommendations form much of the basis of current public personnel thought and were reflected in the 1883 reforms.[10]

Although the experiment had to be abandoned, it whetted the appetites of reformers, and the issue would not die. The ensuing scandals of the Grant administration only helped make civil service reform a more vital political issue. Another supporter of merit, Rutherford B. Hayes, became president in 1877 and also made some tentative moves toward reform. The controversy surrounding his election left him politically weak, however, and he was unable to accomplish much. Indications are that what he did do to institute reform in some departments was more than offset by his lack of effort in others. Furthermore, Hayes's inconsistency in implementing executive orders against assessment (requiring employees to contribute a percentage of their salaries to the political party) and partisan activity leads one to question the sincerity of his commitment to reform.[11]

Nonetheless, the issue of reform was attracting an ever-widening group of supporters. During the late 1870s and early 1880s, various associations favoring civil service reform organized and became vocal. They attempted to pressure political leaders, but more importantly, they tried to educate the public to the evils of spoils. They portrayed the spoils system as one that undermines the work ethic and feeds the avarice of the bad citizen. But somehow, the people still had not become intensely interested, although some public concern was manifested in the elections of presidents committed to reform. With the aid of an increasingly interested press, however, the reformers made their mark on the public and politicians alike.[12]

The assassination of President James A. Garfield became a dramatic symbol of the evils of spoils—it could even lead to murder. The fact that Charles Guiteau, Garfield's assassin, was an unsuccessful seeker of patronage employment gave the reformers the impetus they needed, and that Garfield was a supporter of reform only added to their sense of urgency.

Another political factor favoring reform was the Supreme Court decision in *Ex parte Curtis* in 1882.[13] Congress had passed a law in 1876 that prohibited the assessment of government workers. This practice, which still exists in some jurisdictions, involves a "contribution," or kickback, of a portion of the employee's salary to his or her political party organization or other benefactor. Obviously, when the patronage system is in use, assessment can be easily enforced: if the employee refuses to "contribute," he or she is removed. In any case, assessment became a scandal when Newton Curtis, a Treasury Department employee and treasurer of the New York Republican party, was brought to trial for violating the 1876 law. The Supreme Court upheld his conviction and the law, and reform efforts could only gain from the decision.

In addition, the congressional elections of 1882 made the Republicans reflect on the political consequences of reform. Republican fortunes slipped badly in the elections, and a continuation of this trend would mean loss of the White House in 1884, the loss of power to appoint public servants, and possible large-scale purges of Republican officeholders. Congressional Republicans thus saw the wisdom of supporting reform.

As a result of the aforementioned political forces and the persistent efforts of reformers, the Pendleton Civil Service Act became law on January 16, 1883. The act created a personnel system based on the merit concept and required the formulation of rules and regulations by which all personnel activities would be conducted. It took a long time and the assassination of a president, but Congress had acted. Now the character of the public service underwent another revolution.

Consolidation of Reform Efforts

Passage of the Pendleton Act did not bring an end to the spoils system, however, nor did it mean that reform became a dead issue. The public servants covered by the act amounted to only about 10 percent of public employees in the national government, and so for that 10 percent, employment decisions were now supposed to be based on merit considerations. To implement the system, the president was authorized to appoint a bipartisan civil service commission. The basic elements of the civil service included competitive examinations, lateral entry, neutrality, and the prohibition of political party assessments of civil servants, among many other features. Apparently some supporters of reform expected the public service to become the domain of the aristocracy once again,[14] but this did not happen, partly because of the act's provisions and partly because of its gradual application. The greater attention to educational criteria for employment, though, gave an advantage to the upper socioeconomic groups.

In passing the Pendleton Act, Congress attempted to exert control over the personnel system of the United States government. Because the president is given executive authority by the Constitution, the constitutionality of congressional control was questioned. Consequently, Congress made the legislation permissive, meaning that the president could provide for establishment of the merit system but was not directed to do so.[15] Certainly, the political squabbles between the president and Congress had an impact, but the realities of the constitutional provisions had to be accommodated.

Each of the act's major provisions had political implications. The first, authorizing rather than mandating presidential action on the matter, has already been discussed in terms of the conflict between the president and Congress. Open competitive exams and lateral entry may be seen as adherence to the democratic tradition of equality. The reformers were actually interested in adopting the British system requiring entry at the bottom and promotion from within. But because the egalitarian tradition of the United States was inconsistent with such a provision, the open system was adopted. Some suggest that the Democrats put the Republicans on the defensive and forced them to adopt the open system for fear of being branded as undemocratic by the press and the public.[16] Certainly this is true, though the Democrats were not entirely altruistic. They were doubtlessly concerned with being able to balance the public service in their favor should they win the presidency in 1884, as they did. It would be difficult to reward Democratic partisans if the current Republican president were to choose all of the high-level public servants. But with lateral entry, any vacancies at higher levels could be given to the Democrats within the limits of the competitive system.

Apportionment among the states of the positions in the Washington offices meant that the constituents of each member of Congress had a realistic chance to obtain employment. The South also was concerned about its inadequate representation in public service positions. And in addition, apportionment helped further integrate the nation by ensuring participation by people from all parts of the country.

Both political parties realized the importance of the provisions regarding extending or reducing the extent of the merit system's coverage. Congress could hardly direct that all public employees be covered, given the constitutional question discussed earlier, and so the extent of coverage was to be determined by the president. Because the president might also abuse this power, especially as a lame duck, he was also authorized to roll back the coverage—a power that has been used very seldom. President William McKinley exercised this power in his first term, precipitating a bitter reaction, and thus others have been reluctant to try it. In contrast, presidents have frequently extended the coverage—particularly at the end of their terms—so that approximately 90 percent of federal government civilian employees are now under some sort of merit system.

It is clear that political considerations affected the decisions to reform the public service in 1883 and have been factors ever since in the system's evolution. David Rosenbloom suggested that the 1883 reform was political, in that its intent was to rescue government from the professional politicians.[17] The conflict between the values of the professional politician and the advocates of strict merit continue to fuel the debate concerning how to make government personnel responsive.

Changing Concerns of the Merit System

Although the Civil Service Commission seemed to have a fairly broad grant of power under the Civil Service Act, it really exercised very little, devoting most of its early years to screening applicants.[18] Considering the political climate in which it was born, it is little wonder that the presidents and the commission moved cautiously. Remember that Congress created the new system more because of public sentiment and the reformers' pressure than because it was committed to reform. Gradually, however, the commission gained prestige and influence and became the major force in public personnel policies. When Theodore Roosevelt became president in 1901, the civil service system had a friend in its chief executive. A former commissioner of civil service, Roosevelt did much to improve the service's image and to increase its coverage. From that day on, with minor exceptions, the commission's position has remained strong.

During the late nineteenth and early twentieth centuries, many changes in society and politics brought adaptive changes in the civil service system. In 1883 the jobs of public servants were still primarily clerkships, but the Industrial Revolution had changed technology, and the post–Civil War era brought on a period of intensified development in the economy. Technological advances and their consequences made new demands on the political system and resulted in an ever-larger public service. Jobs became more specialized and with this development came the need for yet another specialty—the personnel administrator.

The new system was also faced with constantly changing political forces. Workers' movements resulting in union organizations had an early impact on the public service—the National Association of Letter Carriers, for instance, was organized in 1889. Concern with employees' welfare became another issue to be considered. As a result, there has been a gradual development and extension of benefits, so that today federal government employees have one of the best benefit packages available.

We pointed out earlier that the spoils system at the national level followed its development in state and local jurisdictions. When the federal government instituted reforms, however, most state and local governments were slow to follow its lead.[19] In 1883 New York adopted the first state civil service law, but only one other state, Massachusetts, enacted such a law before the turn of the century. In 1884 Albany, New York, became the first city to create a civil service system, and several other cities and one county (Cook County, Illinois) followed suit during the 1880s and 1890s. Coverage usually applied to clerical workers and the uniformed services of police and fire.

With the muckrakers' attention focused on corruption in municipal government in the early years of the twentieth century, the pressure for reform grew. Similar exposure of patronage abuse in state governments had the same effect. Many state and municipal governments, therefore, developed civil service systems, beginning in 1900 and continuing through the 1920s. Although the scope of these reforms was usually limited, these actions did herald an era of major change in state and local personnel practices. The Great Depression of 1929, however, brought a precipitous halt to most of the reform efforts. State and local governments cut back their funding of such programs as they attempted to cope with other, more pressing problems relating to their citizens' physical well-being.

The national government was consolidating its reform effort, and the United States Civil Service Commission gradually centralized its authority. Established to protect the neutrality of the federal government service, the commission performed the major personnel functions and also monitored agencies' activities to see that they abided by the new civil service rules and regulations.

The Depression brought changes to the federal government service, just as it did with state and local governments. President Franklin Roosevelt, in his efforts to create programs to deal with the economic crisis, felt that the already-established bureaucracy was not flexible and adaptable enough to act quickly and that speedy action was required if people were to receive the help they needed to avoid total disaster. Convinced that the existing agencies were not up to this task, Roosevelt persuaded Congress to create many agencies outside the civil service. Although most of the employees of these agencies were "blanketed in" (given civil service coverage by executive order), they did represent a loss of control by the Civil Service Commission.

Roosevelt also directed individual departments and agencies to create their own personnel units. These units eventually performed the majority of personnel actions for their agencies. Another factor leading to the decentralization of personnel activities was the World War II war effort. The Civil Service Commission was unable to keep up with the demands made by the new and rapidly growing agencies, resulting in relative independence for the departments.

Although there were efforts to reestablish the commission's authority, decentralization characterized the personnel function after the war. Individual departments became increasingly responsible for implementing personnel policies. The role of the Civil Service Commission also changed, becoming that of a policymaker, a provider of technical and support services, and a monitor of personnel activities. These changes in its role remain today, even though the old commission was abolished, and a new organization was created in its place.

Other changes as well were occurring in personnel activities during this period. During the 1930s and 1940s, federal government policy began to impose limits on state and local levels. The Social Security Act of 1935 created programs in which national government funding assisted state governments in some programs. The act required that such programs be efficiently administered, but there were no provisions for enforcing such a vague prescription. In 1940 the act was amended to permit specific federal personnel requirements in state and local programs utilizing federal monies under the Social Security Act. Over the years, Congress has provided for similar regulations requiring merit systems in other federal programs. Currently, there is a uniform set of merit principle guidelines for federally funded projects.

Another 1940 provision, an amendment to the 1939 Hatch Act, prohibited most political activity by employees of state and local government programs funded by federal monies. These provisions were repealed in 1974, but most states adopted their own statutes restricting partisan political activities; therefore, the federal repeal has not resulted in much change for employees.

Although the trend of the 1980s has been to reduce the intrusion of federal government into state and local activities, there are still restrictions that apply to their personnel policies. Nondiscrimination and equal employment opportunity are just some of the conditions attached to federal monies at present.

During the 1930s and 1940s, there was a slow but steady growth in the number of states and municipalities adopting civil service systems. During the 1950s, however, the pace quickened, and partly because of the prodding of the federal government's grant-in-aid restrictions on personnel, thirty-five states now have statewide systems, and the remaining fifteen have less comprehensive systems. The municipalities have also enacted provisions of civil service systems in increasing numbers. The counties remain dominated by patronage systems, however.

The federal government public service continued to change during this period. The Hatch Act of 1939 gave legislative force to the Civil Service Commission's prohibitions on political activity, and the Ramspeck Act of 1940 prohibited discrimination in the personnel process. Preference was given to veterans in the Veteran's Preference Act of 1944, and the Government Employees Training Act of 1958 focused attention on the need for employees' continued personal growth. In recent years, personnel systems have been challenged by developments in collective bargaining, equal employment opportunity, productivity improvement, intergovernmental concerns, and continually changing political environments.

Civil Service Reform Act of 1978 and Beyond

Ever since the Pendleton Civil Service Act was passed, there have been suggestions for its reform. Although many changes have been made over the years, there was no comprehensive reform of civil service until the enactment of the Civil Service Reform Act of 1978. Fulfilling an election campaign promise to reform government so as to improve its efficiency, President Jimmy Carter pushed strongly for adoption of the Reform Act. Along with the act, two reorganization plans were approved by Congress to reorganize the Civil Service Commission and to shift some of its responsibilities to the Equal Employment Opportunity Commission.[20] These reforms took effect in January 1979.

The legislation divided the Civil Service Commission's activities between the new Office of Personnel Management (OPM) and the Merit Systems Protection Board (MSPB). The Federal Labor Relations Authority (FLRA) was also created to monitor federal labor-management relations policies. This division of responsibilities reflects the objections of many, especially employee organizations, to one organization having policymaking, implementing, and reviewing authority. Employees often viewed the commission as representing management and did not feel comfortable in approaching it with complaints or for review of personnel actions. Under the new system, the Office of Personnel Management, headed by a director and a deputy director appointed by the president, has responsibility for general personnel policy development for federal employees, as well as for examinations, personnel investigations, evaluation of personnel programs, and training and development. The OPM will also offer technical assistance to departments and will administer retirement and benefit programs for federal employees.

The independent Merit Systems Protection Board is supposed to protect employees against unfair personnel actions and other abuses. It also is to see that the merit system itself is protected and makes annual reports to Congress on the merit system operations. Employees are able to appeal personnel actions to the MSPB, and it has the authority to institute actions to correct abuses. An important feature of the reform is that the Special Counsel established within the MSPB has the power to investigate the activities of agencies and officials. The Special Counsel can also ask the MSPB to take action against those who violate the merit system laws.

The Federal Labor Relations Authority monitors federal collective bargaining activity, such as the establishment of bargaining units and collective bargaining elections, and works with departments and agencies on labor-management relations activities. A general counsel in the FLRA investigates and prosecutes unfair labor practices. The Federal Service Impasses Panel remains an independent agency to help resolve negotiation impasses.

Several features of the Reform Act dealt with personnel policy issues. For example, the OPM is authorized to delegate many of its functions to operating departments, thus continuing the post-1933 trend toward decentralizing personnel functions. The Senior Executive Service (SES) created by the act permits some high-level managers to be assigned where needed so as to maximize the use of their talents. They are also eligible for substantial pay increases for meritorious service. Indeed, merit became the basis for pay increases for other managers in the federal service as well.

The legislation also streamlined the process for dismissing incompetent employees. In addition, whistle blowers, that is, employees who expose illegal activities or mismanagement in their agencies, are supposed to be protected against reprisals by their superiors. One of the act's most important features is that it put into law some of the items that previously existed only by executive order or through Civil Service Commission policy. One such provision spells out and protects public employees' collective bargaining rights. Another lists specific merit principles and prohibited practices (see Table 2-1).

The Reform Act was intended to improve the federal personnel system in general and the performance of public employees in particular. Many state and local governments were considering reform at the same time, and many others acted after the national government passed its legislation. The national law thus became a model for state and local governments.[21]

Numerous political forces combined to bring about the reform efforts, popular disenchantment with government and a president willing to push for such legislation being among the most important.[22] Also influential were the problems created by the Nixon administration's attempt to politicize the public service and the changes in congressional leadership that made it more receptive to reform. The appointment of a prestigious task force to study the civil service and make recommendations gave the effort additional credibility. Similar forces at the state and local levels, along with fiscal retrenchment, led to efforts to improve their public services.

Continuing Concerns in Personnel Management

Many issues addressed by various reform efforts continue to challenge public personnel management. Among the most prominent are the conflict between legislatures and executives for control of the bureaucracy, and the role of professionals and spoils versus merit.[23]

LEGISLATIVE-EXECUTIVE CONFLICTS

Legislators and elected executives constantly strive to control many aspects of the personnel function. Executives traditionally view government personnel as instruments through which their policy perspectives can be translated into government action. In reality, most elected political executives complain that civil service personnel actually impede their efforts at fulfilling the campaign promises supposedly desired by the voters. Newly elected presidents, governors, and mayors customarily deplore the bureaucracy's lack of response to their policy directives. As such, executives often view the merit system as decreasing their ability to control policy and see the spoils system as augmenting that power.[24]

Legislative bodies, however, wish to control policy too. They see influence over the personnel system as one way to do this or at least to weaken the executive's ability to exercise such power. The close relationship of legislative committees to administrative agencies serves to ensure legislative influence over agency personnel. In addition, wedges are often driven between lower-level officials and their superiors by committees insisting on hearing employees' personal views, as opposed to official policy.[25]

Lower-level bureaucrats are often protected by legislative committees or influential members of the legislative body. The State Department, for example, tried for years to change passport regulations, but Frances Knight, the director of the Passport Office, took a very cautious approach to easing the restrictions. Furthermore, even a hint at replacing her was invariably met by pressure from conservative supporters in Congress who viewed her as a protector of United States security. Although Knight did institute some changes, she was able to withstand this pressure for most of the Cold War era and beyond, because congressional support insulated her from her nominal superiors. J. Edgar Hoover, longtime director of the Federal Bureau of Investigation (FBI), is another example of how such protection can develop.

As noted in our discussion of the Civil Service Act of 1883, legislative and executive conflict over which will control the public service resulted in compromises in the establishment of the civil service system. A similar conflict arose in the consideration of the Civil Service Reform Act of 1978. The president was definitely interested in exerting more control over the personnel function and wanted the OPM to answer to the president. But Congress, of course, was wary and built in some safeguards against too much presidential control. Thus the creation of the MSPB was one way of allaying some of Congress' fears. The differing concerns of executives and legislators will continue to be a source of conflict as public personnel systems continue to evolve.

Table 2–1 Provisions of the Civil Service Reform Act of 1978

Merit System Principles	Prohibited Personnel Practices
Personnel practices and actions in the federal government require:	*Officials and employees who are authorized to take personnel actions are prohibited from:*

• Recruitment from all segments of society, and selection and advancement on the basis of ability, knowledge, and skills, under fair and open competition.

• Fair and equitable treatment in all personnel management matters, without regard to politics, race, color, religion, national origin, sex, marital status, age, or handicapping condition, and with proper regard for individual privacy and constitutional rights.

• Equal pay for work of equal value, considering both national and local rates paid by private employers, with incentives and recognition for excellent performance.

• High standards of integrity, conduct, and concern for the public interest.

• Efficient and effective use of the Federal work force.

• Retention of employees who perform well, correcting the performance of those whose work is inadequate, and separation of those who cannot or will not meet required standards.

• Improved performance through effective education and training.

• Protection of employees from arbitrary action, personal favoritism, or political coercion.

• Protection of employees against reprisal for lawful disclosures of information.

• Discrimination against any employee or applicant.

• Soliciting or considering any recommendation on a person who requests or is being considered for a personnel action unless the material is an evaluation of the person's work performance, ability, aptitude, or general qualifications, or character, loyalty, and suitability.

• Using official authority to coerce political actions, to require political contributions, or to retaliate for refusal to do these things.

• Willfully deceiving or obstructing an individual as to his or her right to compete for Federal employment.

• Influencing anyone to withdraw from competition, whether to improve or worsen the prospects of any applicant.

• Granting any special preferential treatment or advantage not authorized by law to a job applicant or employee.

• Appointing, employing, promoting, or advancing relatives in their agencies.

• Taking or failing to take a personnel action as a reprisal against employees who exercise their appeal rights; refuse to engage in political activity; or lawfully disclose violations of law, rule, or regulation, or mismanagement, gross waste of funds, abuse of

Merit System Principles	Prohibited Personnel Practices
	authority, or a substantial and specific danger to public health or safety. • Taking or failing to take any other personnel action violating a law, rule, or regulation directly related to merit system principles.

Source: U.S. Civil Service Commission, *Introducing the Civil Service Reform Act* (Washington, D.C.: U.S. Government Printing Office, November 1978), p. 2.

PROFESSIONALS: INHERITORS OF THE SYSTEM

President Jackson characterized the work of government as being simple enough for any citizen to perform and he was not far from the truth, because at the time most government work was simple clerical tasks. However, today even clerical work requires complex skills and responsibilities. Even more to the point, modern society requires government activities calling for a high degree of expertise in practically every field of endeavor. The challenge of creating a personnel system capable of satisfying those needs is great. As the public service has become more specialized, it also has had to deal with professionalization in the personnel activities themselves.

Professionalization occurs with the development of specialized bodies of knowledge and standards for applying that expertise. Modern society has produced many new professions, along with which come professional associations that strive for the best possible performance of the specialty. The associations enable professionals to meet with and learn from fellow specialists and to keep up with recent developments in the field. Professional groups also develop codes of ethics or conduct. The professionalization of public personnel thereby has the potential of benefiting the public service both by disseminating knowledge and establishing standards. But there are costs as well.

Professionalism is normally characterized by (1) decisions being made on the basis of criteria that are universal and not dependent on the particular situation, (2) specialization, (3) neutrality, (4) success being measured by performance, (5) the elimination of self-interest in the decision-making process, and (6) self-control over professional activities.[26] The first five of these characteristics are beneficial to the public service and consistent with most of its features. The last, self-control, however, is diametrically opposed to the principle that public personnel be accountable to the public and its elected representatives.

Frederick Mosher suggested that professionals have assumed control over the public agencies in which they work, developed an elite core within the agency to exercise that control, dominated many personnel policies, and provided protection for the members of the profession.[27] Let us look at these effects and others.

As professionals became more numerous in public agencies, their efforts turned from striving for the best performance to a contest for power.[28] Thus the emphasis is now often on gaining policy control through domination of the agency. Professional groups tend to establish their own territorial jurisdiction in agencies and draw up operating procedures and approaches based on their expertise.[29] For example, the biologists and engineers in an environmental group may compete for control. Although their expertise is beneficial to the agency, there are also problems in permitting professional organizations to have control. An elite not accountable to the general public is in control under such circumstances, and so questions arise over the relationship of the public service to the rest of the political system. In public education, for instance, teachers' associations have been successful in establishing the criteria by which personnel decisions are made and persuading school districts and state education agencies to accept them. Many of the current criticisms of the quality of public education are directed at the professionals who control them. Many critics feel that the professional education establishment seems more concerned about its own welfare than the welfare of those they are supposed to be educating.

Personnel systems are affected to the extent that professional associations dominate various personnel policies as they gain effective control over agency activities. The professional association may influence recruitment or selection in agency employment by dominating the process of establishing qualifications for applicants. Thus the recognition or certification of programs and projects as meeting professional standards normally depends on the agency's hiring personnel with recognized professional training or experience. Such efforts restrict the flexibility and weaken the authority of personnel agencies and administrators.

Professional associations also emphasize the profession's status and autonomy. Professionals tend to respond to the pressure of the professional organization and their professional peers rather than to the agency's authority structure. The effect can be to undermine the agency's hierarchical lines of authority. In many ways the professional associations become protective shields for their members and theoretically ward off the formal and legal control.[30] Related to the issue of control is employees' loyalty to their agencies. The more highly professionalized people are, the less loyal to their employers and the more loyal to professional associations and standards they will become.[31] Often such employees view the employing organization as an instrument for advancement and move from one organization to another as they advance professionally. In such a case, they may also pursue their personal interests at the expense of the public and the public service. In addition, intense specialization often produces a very narrow view on the part of individual employees. They become so preoccupied with their particular field of interest that the organization's larger work suffers from a lack of coordination and interchange among different specialties. Personnel activities, particularly effective supervision, are difficult under such circumstances.

With its emphasis on performance and merit, professionalization is antithetical to spoils and patronage and thus helps further insulate the personnel system from partisan politics. Similarly, professionalization conflicts with the preferential treatment of individuals on bases other than merit. For example, veterans' preference policies are inconsistent with basic professional standards.

Partly as a result of professionalization, the public service itself has attempted to improve the performance of public employees. Governments help their employees adapt to modern society through executive seminars, executive assignment programs, training and development programs, and utilization of programs offered through other institutions such as universities, professional associations, and private consultants. Such programs expose public servants to a high level of professional training and help improve the quality of public service. There is little doubt that professionalization will continue. The challenge for public personnel managers is ensuring that it works in the public interest.[32] Personnel administrators have their own professional associations and thus are able to see firsthand some of the effects of professionalization.

SPOILS VERSUS MERIT

Another issue that affects the personnel function is the conflict between spoils and merit as bases for personnel actions. The main distinction between the two systems is that the spoils approach emphasizes loyalty, and the merit concept stresses competence or expertise. Each system needs both attributes, however, if it is to work effectively.

Because the abuses of the spoils system led to political corruption, it is viewed as an evil, and there is little appreciation of the system's positive contributions. Yet the spoils system was largely responsible for democratizing the public service. By breaking the aristocracy's hold on government jobs, the system brought people from all walks of life and from all areas of the nation into the public service. It provided a mechanism for integrating and unifying the political system. The epitome of this functional role was Lincoln's use of patronage during the Civil War, when partisan appointments were instrumental in gaining support for a controversial cause.

The spoils system also helped build and unify the political parties in the United States. Voters were attracted by the prospect of patronage rewards, and party finances were strengthened through the use of assessments. In addition, with the buildup of party machines, the spoils system aided in the political socialization of various ethnic groups in the larger cities and provided many of the social services now performed by governmental agencies.

Jacksonian Democracy's focus on egalitarianism somehow became obscured in the quest for patronage positions, and in an ironic twist, egalitarianism also became an important issue in the reform movement's arguments. The abuse of the spoils system pointed up some of its costs. The constantly changing bureaucracy led to gross inefficiencies, some incompetence, and even chaos and insecurity for the public employee. In addition, the president and Congress found themselves constantly at odds over appointments, meaning that government was often at a standstill. More importantly, the president squandered much time and energy worrying about whom to appoint to what position. Office seekers arrived in never-ending streams, and whether or not jobs were available, the president wasted valuable time dealing with them. The quality of social services provided by political machines was lessened by the corruption and partiality of the political and administrative processes.

The spoils system inevitably led to favoritism and inequity in the treatment of the public, and so the reformers tried to neutralize and democratize the public service. The civil service system was heralded as the savior of our political order, and it created a neutral public service in which employees are chosen and dealt with on the basis of their competence and ability to perform. The merit system was also supposed to foster egalitarianism, in that everyone would have a chance to compete—not just those who happened to support the political leaders. A major concern of the reformers was to bring morality back to the public service. The merit system would free public servants from the control of the evil politicians and the machines and permit the bureaucracy to focus its attention on the job of serving the public. The merit system led to vast changes in bureaucracy and aided in reviving the prestige of the public service. Ultimately, however, problems were to be found with it as well.

One of the unintended consequences of the merit system is that it weakens the supervisor's authority. Because the supervisor does not directly control the selection and removal process, and as protections for employee job security grow, the employee will gain a degree of independence. This criticism is frequently exaggerated, but it is worth considering. An allied criticism is that under a merit system, the bureaucracy is not as responsive to the people, because their representatives have less control when they must consider factors other than loyalty in making appointments. Of course, others argue that the bureaucracy is more responsive because it is more competent and better able to serve the "real" needs of the people.

A major criticism of the merit system is that it has strayed from the egalitarian concept, just as the spoils system did. The examination process obviously eliminates some people from consideration and is seen as a positive instrument for selecting the best qualified. But questions are raised about the appropriateness of the exams. Do they measure the qualities required for successful performance? Similarly, questions are raised about the appropriateness of the credentials required for positions. These issues are central to a merit system and are the cause of many conflicts.

It is an extreme oversimplification to distinguish between spoils and merit as the difference between evil and good, but unfortunately, many people do just that. In reality, each is a product of particular political and social forces. Neither can provide effective bureaucracy without some cost. Although the trend in the United States has been to move toward a neutral merit bureaucracy, patronage is still important at all levels of government. The use of patronage has been adapted to changing conditions and demands, just as the merit system has been adapted.[33] Some argue that the merit system has created a politics of its own, one that seeks support for its programs, agency autonomy, professional association interests, and clientele interests.[34] These interests and groups play the game of politics and insist that the spoils be theirs rather than the political party's. But regardless of how the system is perceived, it is certain to change in response to demands and pressures from the political environment.

Summary

The conflict between spoils and merit principles has been an enduring issue in the public service. Merit systems were developed originally to rid public personnel of political patronage. Consequently, the primary emphasis of merit personnel systems has been on policing personnel actions. Most personnel departments spend much of their time making sure that others comply with personnel policies, rules, and regulations. Although changes are occurring, such policing is still prominent in the activities of personnel administrators, particularly at the state and local levels.

Although policing is still important, as in equal employment opportunity programs, merit systems are being confronted by many other challenges and, in the process, are undergoing change. To a great extent, personnel agencies are providing assistance to other agencies so that they can comply with personnel policies and also improve the quality of the public service. Central personnel agencies offer technical assistance, training programs, and services for labor-management relations, among others. Through such activities, personnel administrators can reduce the tension between them and department managers so that they can work together to accomplish the government's objectives. Actually, cooperation seems to be more evident in recent years, as the central personnel function has centered on policy development, review, and technical assistance, and individual agencies have been performing more of the day-to-day personnel functions. The Civil Service Reform Act of 1978 and its progeny at the state and local level have accentuated this trend.

Other concerns affecting personnel management at all levels of government include collective bargaining, equal employment opportunity, productivity, intergovernmental activities, contracting for services, fiscal limitations, and demands from the physical environment. The rest of the book will examine the impact of these issues on public personnel administration.

NOTES

1. Two who emphasize other significant breaks are Paul P. Van Riper, *History of the United States Civil Service* (New York: Harper & Row, 1958); and Frederick C. Mosher, *Democracy and the Public Service*, 2d. ed. (New York: Oxford University Press, 1982).

2. See Herbert Kaufman, "The Growth of the Federal Personnel Service," in Wallace Sayre, ed., *The Federal Government Service: Its Character, Prestige, and Problems*, 2nd ed. (Englewood Cliffs, N.J.: Prentice-Hall, 1965), pp. 7–69, at pp. 12–14; Van Riper, *History of the United States Civil Service*, pp. 20–22; and Mosher, *Democracy and the Public Service*, pp. 55–61.

3. See Leonard D. White, *The Federalists: A Study in Administrative History* (New York: Macmillan, 1948), pp. 257–263. White's analysis provides much of the background for the discussion of Washington and the Federalists. Readers wanting a detailed discussion of the early development of the public service should consult this work.

4. Van Riper, *History of the United States Civil Service*, p. 27.

5. Leonard D. White, *The Jeffersonians: A Study in Administrative History 1801–1829* (New York: Macmillan, 1961), provides an excellent review of public personnel policies in the period under consideration. See pp. 347–368 in particular.

6. For a colorful account of the events, see Carl Russell Fish, *The Civil Service and the Patronage* (New York: Russell & Russell, 1963, originally pub. 1904), pp. 105–113.

7. The information on which this section is based comes largely from Fish, ibid., pp. 169–177.

8. Ibid., pp. 186–197. For the most complete analysis of the movement for reform, see Ari Hoogenboom, *Outlawing the Spoils: A History of the Civil Service Reform Movement 1865–1883* (Urbana: University of Illinois Press, 1961).

9. Fish, *The Civil Service and the Patronage*, p. 213.

10. For a detailed account of the Grant commission's recommendations and actions, see Lionel V. Murphy, "The First Federal Civil Service Commission: 1871–1875," *Public Personnel Review*, 3 (January, July, and October 1942), 29–39, 218–231, 299–323.

11. Hoogenboom, *Outlawing the Spoils*, pp. 143–178, provides an in-depth analysis of Hayes' efforts.

12. For some excellent statements of proponents and opponents of reform, see the collection of periodical articles of the times in Ari Hoogenboom, ed., *Spoilsmen and Reformers*, (Chicago: Rand McNally, 1964). The intensity of feeling is apparent in the words of the writers themselves. An interesting account of press interest may be found in Charles J. Nelson, "The Press and Civil Service Reform," *Civil Service Journal*, 13 (April-June 1973), 1–3.

13. 106 U.S. 371; 27 L. Ed. 232 (1882).

14. Ari Hoogenboom, "The Pendleton Act and the Civil Service," *American Historical Review*, 64 (1958–59), 301–318, at p. 312. Hoogenboom, *Outlawing the Spoils*, p. 278, gives statistics on coverage.

15. Rocco C. Siciliano, "The Federal Personnel System Under Scrutiny," in Thomas Page, ed., *The Public Personnel Agency and the Chief Executive*, Personnel Report no. 601 (Chicago: Public Personnel Association, n.d.), pp. 12–18, at pp. 13–14, examines the issue and its effects.

16. See Hoogenboom, *Outlawing the Spoils*, p. 241. Van Riper, *History of the U.S. Civil Service*, has an informative chapter on the general issue of accommodation of the European import to our political culture, pp. 96–112.

17. David H. Rosenbloom, "Politics and Public Personnel Administration: The Legacy of 1883," in David H. Rosenbloom, ed., *Centenary Issues of the Pendleton Act of 1883: The Problematic Legacy of Civil Service Reform* (New York: Marcel Dekker, 1982), pp. 1–10.

18. Hoogenboom, "The Pendleton Act and the Civil Service," p. 305.

19. For a review of state and local developments, see Albert H. Aronson, "State and Local Personnel Administration," in Frank J. Thompson, ed., *Classics of Public Personnel Policy* (Oak Park, Ill.: Moore, 1979), pp. 102–111, based on material from U.S. Civil Service Commission, *Biography of an Ideal* (Washington, D.C.: U.S. Government Printing Office, 1974), pp. 127–135, 138–144. This section draws heavily on Aronson's account.

20. A more detailed description of the effects of the Reform Act is in U.S. Civil Service Commission, *Introducing the Civil Service Reform Act* (Washington, D.C.: U.S. Government Printing Office, November, 1978).

21. For a review of some of the efforts at the state and local levels, see U.S. Civil Service Commission, *Conference Report on Public Personnel Management Reform* (Washington, D.C.: USCSC, Bureau of Intergovernmental Personnel Programs, 1978); and periodic updates in *Intergovernmental Personnel Notes*, published bimonthly by the Office of Personnel Management.

22. For a review of the various forces, see Steven Knudsen, Larry Jakus, and Maida Metz, "The Civil Service Reform Act of 1978," *Public Personnel Management*, 8, no. 3 (May-June 1979), 170–181.

23. Chester A. Newland, "Crucial Issues for Public Personnel Professionals," *Public Personnel Management*, 13 (Spring 1984), 15–46, raises other issues and challenges for public personnel management. Several others react to Newland's ideas in the ensuing pages. Similarly, Muriel M. Morse, "Conflict and Change in Personnel Management—An International Challenge," *Public Personnel Management*, 13 (Spring 1984), 7–14, suggests the challenges ahead.

24. This and the following discussions are based largely on Harvey C. Mansfield, "Political Parties, Patronage, and the Federal Government Service," in Sayre, ed., *The Federal Government Service*, pp. 114–162, at pp. 140–149; and Herman Miles Somers, "The President, Congress, and the Federal Government Service," in Sayre, ed., ibid., pp. 70–113 at pp. 73–86.

25. Somers, "The President, Congress, and the Federal Government Service," p. 86.

26. For elaboration of these characteristics, see Peter M. Blau and W. Richard Scott, *Formal Organizations: A Comparative Approach* (San Francisco: Chandler, 1962), pp. 60–63.

27. Mosher, *Democracy and the Public Service*, pp. 119–120. Also see p. 230. The following discussion is based on much of Chapters 5 and 6 of this seminal work.

28. See David Schuman, *Bureaucracies, Organization, and Administration: A Political Primer* (New York: Macmillan, 1976), pp. 170–173.

29. Harold Seidman, *Politics, Position, and Power: The Dynamics of Federal Organization*, 3rd ed. (New York: Oxford University Press, 1980), pp. 156–162, discusses these issues.

30. Schuman, *Bureaucracies, Organization, and Administration*, pp. 172–173, George Frederick Goerl, "Cybernetics, Professionalization, and Knowledge Management: An Exercise in Assumptive Theory," *Public Administration Review*, 35 (November-December 1975), 581–588, also discusses these issues.

31. Blau and Scott, *Formal Organizations*, pp. 64–67, describe the studies of this issue.

32. Frederick C. Mosher and Richard Stillman, Jr., "A Symposium: The Professions in Government, Introduction," *Public Administration Review*, 37 (November-December 1977), 631–633, traces the professionalism of the service. Richard L. Schott, "Public Administration As a Profession," *Public Administration Review*, 36 (May-June 1976), 253–259, discusses the issue from a more general perspective. An in-depth discussion of the issue can also be found in Don L. Bowen, ed. *Public Service Professional Associations and the Public Interest* (Philadelphia: American Academy of Political and Social Science, 1973).

33. For a particularly good analysis of changing terms of patronage, see Frank J. Sorauf, "The Silent Revolution in Patronage," *Public Administration Review*, 20 (Winter 1960), 28–34.

34. Kaufman, "The Growth of the Federal Personnel Service," pp. 59–69.

SUGGESTED READINGS

Bowman, James S., ed. "Symposium on Civil Service Reform." *Review of Public Personnel Administration*, 2 (Spring 1982), 1–134; and 2 (Summer 1982), 1–92.

Ealy, Steven D. "Reform of the Georgia State Merit System," *Review of Public Personnel Administration*, 1 (Summer 1981), 33–50.

Hoogenboom, Ari. *Outlawing the Spoils: A History of the Civil Service Reform Movement 1865–1883*. Urbana: University of Illinois Press, 1961.

Mosher, Frederick C. *Democracy and the Public Service*, 2d ed. New York: Oxford University Press, 1982.

Nalbandian, John, and Donald Klingner. "The Politics of Public Personnel Administration: Towards Theoretical Understanding." *Public Administration Review*, 41 (September-October 1982), 541–549.

Panetta, Leon E., and Peter Gall. *Bring Us Together.* Philadelphia: Lippincott, 1971.

Rosen, Bernard. "Merit and the President's Plan for Changing the Civil Service System." *Public Administration Review,* 38 (July-August 1978), 301–304.

Rosenbloom, David H., ed. *Centenary Issues of the Pendleton Act of 1883: The Problematic Legacy of Civil Service Reform.* New York: Marcel Dekker, 1982.

Sayre, Wallace, ed. *The Federal Government Service: Its Character, Prestige, and Problems.* 2nd ed. Englewood Cliffs, N.J.: Prentice-Hall, 1965.

Smits, William H., Jr. "Personnel Administration—A Viable Function in Government?" *Public Personnel Management,* 11 (Summer 1982), 91–103.

Sorauf, Frank J. "The Silent Revolution in Patronage." *Public Administration Review,* 20 (Winter 1960), 28–34.

Titlow, Richard E. *Americans Import Merit: Origins of the United States Civil Service and the Influence of the British Model.* Washington, D.C.: University Press of America, 1979.

Tolchin, Martin, and Susan Tolchin. *Political Patronage from the Club House to the White House.* New York: Vintage Books, 1971.

Van Riper, Paul P. *History of the United States Civil Service.* New York: Harper & Row, 1958.

Weisband, Edward, and Thomas M. Franck. *Resignation in Protest.* New York: Penguin, 1975.

Case 2.1: A Responsive Personnel System

Marjorie Good ran for mayor because she felt that the city government was responding to too many special interests and was not concerned with the general public. Having had a successful career in business, she was convinced that she could change things in city hall. Furthermore, as president of a major high tech engineering and development corporation, she had demonstrated her outstanding management skills and ran a productive organization.

Upon being elected to the mayor's office, Good had to devise a plan for changing the way the city government was run. Being busy with many issues, she decided to establish task forces for specific areas of concern. She selected you to chair the task force on civil service reform. Before appointing the rest of the task force, she wants your advice on what she should expect when reviewing and recommending changes in personnel policies. Her major aim is to put the city government on a basis similar to that of a business. She also wants your advice on what types of people should be appointed to the task force.

INSTRUCTIONS:

Present your recommendations to Mayor Good. Explain what issues are likely to arise in reviewing and reorganizing the personnel system. What advice do you have for the mayor? Who should she appoint to the task force? Justify your recommendations.

Case 2.2: The Prison Director

John Scurry assumed the job as director of the state prison system amid a great deal of concern about the problems associated with corrections. With the state's tough stance against crime, the prison population was increasing at a rapid rate, but the facilities remained the same. The result was a major overcrowding problem which was leading to many other problems.

In appointing Scurry, Governor Hobit praised him as being a very progressive administrator who could solve the corrections problem for the state. Everything went well for a few months, but then minor changes began to emerge. When hired, Scurry was assured by the governor that he would be strongly supported in his efforts to develop innovative programs to rehabilitate inmates who demonstrated such a potential. Also, the governor voiced strong support of new facilities to ease the crowding problem.

The governor's support was important to the new director, who had a strong reputation for inmate-oriented programs that worked. As election time came closer, the state legislature focused a lot of attention on the prison system and its many problems. Because no new funds had been made available for constructing new facilities, the overcrowding problem became increasingly worse, and there were many discipline problems. There were also several escapes from the facilities. The general public became alarmed, and the prison issue promised to become a major issue in the state election campaign.

The state legislative committee on law and justice held highly publicized hearings on the problems in the state prisons. Scurry was summoned to testify and was berated by several of the majority party members. The governor's party is in the minority in the legislature. The committee's message was clear: Scurry had better clean up the mess in the state prisons and stop creating programs to coddle prisoners, or his agency could forget about any increase in appropriations in the next legislative session. The governor, seeking reelection, has conveniently avoided the issue of prisons to this point.

INSTRUCTIONS:

You are John Scurry. What are your alternatives? What will you choose to do? Why?

3

Alternative Personnel System Models

Although everyone in an organization, especially the managers and supervisors, have personnel responsibilities, certain individuals or units have the primary function of developing and implementing personnel policies. The personnel function may rest with the chief executive officer or with a personnel office, ranging from a few people to a large complex bureaucracy. This chapter will analyze the various bases on which personnel activities may be organized and the alternatives for structuring the personnel function. First we shall explore the function of the personnel office.

Personnel offices are often seen as negative policing agencies that make sure that the operating departments obey rigid rules and procedures. As a result, many department managers view personnel units with suspicion and hostility; rarely do they look to the personnel office as a source of support and assistance. This attitude, though, seems to be changing.[1] The personnel office is supposed to be a service office to the rest of the organization. It performs what is normally referred to as a staff function, as it helps deliver the services of the line departments, which carry out the government's functions.

The personnel office's main service has traditionally been the recruitment of employees. The operating department would requisition persons to fill vacancies. The personnel office would then advertise and interview applicants and administer the appropriate exams in order to certify candidates for selection. Along with these duties, the personnel office would also update the position classification and compensation systems. Its audit and review functions meant policing the departmental activities and often finding problems that would then have to be corrected. Any outside review of activities tends to produce anxieties and suspicion, and personnel offices created both, partly because they often emphasized abiding by "good" rules and regulations while ignoring the need for being flexible and getting things done, which are important to departmental managers.[2]

But the role of personnel offices has changed and expanded greatly in recent years. One change is that personnel is increasingly viewed as supporting all aspects of management.[3] Public sector jurisdictions are becoming more aware of the need for making personnel part of general management and are emulating the private sector by integrating personnel into the overall management function. Tax revolts and fiscal constraints, forcing a more careful use of resources, prod public managers to include personnel administration in decisions involving the largest resource expenditure—the government's personnel. The 1978 Civil Service Reform Act was predicated in large part on President Carter's promise to revamp management at all levels of the federal government. State and local government reforms were stimulated by similar concerns.[4]

Because of these changing attitudes toward the personnel function, many new activities have become the province of the personnel office. Now it must deal with issues of equity in employment, labor-management relations, and the retention and development of good employees. Reform efforts have decentralized many personnel functions, leading to conflicts over the proper role of the central personnel agency and departmental personnel offices. In addition, concerns over the political responsiveness of public servants create new issues. Especially important is maintaining effective services in times of fiscal constraint, including borrowing from the private sector and contracting out services.

Types of Personnel Systems

Fritz Morstein-Marx found four historical patterns in public bureaucracy—those of guardian, caste, patronage, and merit.[5] Muriel Morse observed that in the United States there are also four types of personnel systems, namely, spoils, merit, welfare, and affirmative action.[6] These approaches to bureaucracy and personnel systems help illustrate how the personnel function is organized.

The guardian bureaucracy is based on a predestined selection process in which the guardians protect the good and right. Plato's *Republic* is an example of the guardian approach to bureaucracy. The rulers' bureaucracy maintains the system, which reflects the good society. But determining who is born to rule is not easy. The caste bureaucracy, on the other hand, offers a simpler method of choosing the bureaucracy. People are born into their social caste, and only those of the higher caste can rule. Thus the system normally reflects the society's structure.

The patronage, or spoils, system, of personnel management stems from the model associated with Jacksonian Democracy. In this system, a political leader or other patron rewards supporters by giving jobs to them. Although merit may be taken into account, the primary consideration is whether the potential employee has worked or will work for the interests of those in power. As explained in Chapter 2, many employees in the United States public service are still selected on the basis of spoils. Cabinet members and other high officials are chosen through patronage, as are members of regulatory and other independent agencies and the judiciary in many jurisdictions. Spoils systems also still govern many operations of state and local personnel functions.

Merit personnel systems are common in the United States, at least in theory. Under the merit system, personnel decisions are based on specified standards, qualifications, and performance. Though most civil service systems are justified as merit systems, as was seen in Chapter 2, merit and civil service are not synonymous. The major premises of Weberian bureaucracy (developed by nineteenth-century German sociologist Max Weber) form the basis of merit personnel systems, especially as a career service with fixed salaries, specified selection and training procedures, rules and regulations for all program activities, and evaluation of performance are parts of the personnel function.

Morse's welfare and affirmative action personnel systems are more recent additions to the views of personnel actions. The welfare personnel and affirmative action systems are founded on government employment as the answer to social problems. In the welfare-based approach, government serves as the employer of last resort for people who would not otherwise have jobs, who lack skills, or who are the hard-core unemployed. The public service employment programs of the 1970s, such as the now defunct Comprehensive Employment Training Act (CETA), are examples of such a system.

Similarly, affirmative action personnel systems are based on accomplishing a social purpose. There is much question today as to whether affirmative action will survive the hostile actions of the Reagan administration and recent court decisions. Most jurisdictions, however, do retain equal employment and affirmative action policies, and those policies require that personnel actions be based on broadening the opportunities for groups previously discriminated against. Affirmative action implies some preference for target groups, just as veterans' preference accords advantages to those with military service. Systems based on preferential treatment require that a person's membership in a specified group be taken into account in the employment decision. Other such preferential considerations might include citizenship or residency.

Organizing Personnel Activities

The basic structure of the personnel system in any jurisdiction is based on some form of legal framework. In many cases, the state constitution or local government charters spell out the major requirements for personnel operation. Commonly, such provisions indicate that the public service shall be based on a merit principle and provide for the policymaking and implementation organizations. Whether a civil service commission, single personnel director, or other arrangement will be used is stated, as are the powers and duties of such organizations. In the absence of, or in addition to, constitutional or charter provisions, laws or ordinances establish the system's legal foundation. Executive officers and civil service commissioners or the like also may issue rules and regulations that affect the personnel system's structure. All these bases for establishing the system are related. Normally the constitutional or charter provision grants authority to the legislative body, which then authorizes the personnel or civil service commission to issue rules and regulations. Thus the various elements of the process complement one another in organizing the personnel activities.

There are three organizational questions that must be considered when establishing a personnel system:

1. Is an independent personnel board or commission desirable? If so, what are its powers and functions?
2. Will a central personnel office carry out the personnel activities, or should each department perform its own personnel activities?

3. Should the final personnel authority rest with the chief executive, legislature, or independent personnel board or commission?

The answers to these questions depend on the needs of the individual jurisdictions.[7] Naturally, the needs of a very small unit of government will not be the same as for one with a large employee force. Similarly, jurisdictions with partisan political elections have needs different from those with nonpartisan elections. Each jurisdiction must determine what will work best for it.

A bipartisan or nonpartisan civil service commission or personnel board is the model that dominated public personnel administration at all levels of government in the United States from the 1883 adoption of such a system at the national level. Such agencies generally are responsible for personnel policy development and its implementation. Furthermore, the civil service commission often serves as the appeals board of last resort for employees claiming to have been mistreated by their supervisors and managers. Though the commission commonly has overall responsibility for personnel functions, it is impossible to expect it to carry on the day-to-day activities. Rather, for that purpose, an executive director is usually employed. However, some systems, like that in New York State, designate one member of the commission as the chairperson or president responsible for implementing personnel policies.

The main alternative to the independent commission is creating a central personnel office directly responsible to the chief executive and thus closely connected to the administration's management. The Civil Service Reform Act of 1978 created such an arrangement at the national level, with the new Office of Personnel Management reporting to the president. Many state and local governments instituted similar reforms both before and after the national level did. Where a personnel office reports to the chief executive and supervises the personnel administration, an appeals board of some sort is normally created to review the employee's appeals. The Merit Systems Protection Board at the national level serves such a function. In some instances, a personnel board provides advisory services to the chief executive or the legislative body and approves personnel rules and regulations. New York City, Chicago, and Mesa, Arizona, use this approach, which also is common in state and local government.

Another aspect of personnel organization pertains to whether the function is centralized in one department of personnel or decentralized among the agencies in the jurisdiction. Most systems combine both approaches. In a few places, such as Texas, individual departments still have a great deal of autonomy over most of their personnel activities. There, despite continuing efforts to centralize the system, politics has guaranteed a highly decentralized operation.

The reform movement stimulated by the 1883 Civil Service Act led to the creation of central personnel offices in most large jurisdictions. After World War II, however, the trend was toward decentralizing implementation functions. Recent reforms such as the 1978 Civil Service Reform Act at the national level institutionalize the decentralization. Although central personnel agencies (for example, the OPM) are created to make policy, develop programs, ensure compliance with policy, and provide technical assistance, the operating departments have the day-to-day personnel responsibilities.

Centralizing the personnel function has many advantages. It provides for uniformity in dealing with personnel activities and permits a high degree of specialization in the technical aspects. Economies of scale also result when recruiting, examining, and the like are done for the jurisdiction as a whole. With the increasing influence of labor organizations, a uniformity of policy and procedures also offers support to management, as a lack of uniformity may lower employees' morale and productivity if they evaluate their positions relative to those of others in the organization.

There are also disadvantages to a central office's having all the personnel responsibilities. Critics cite the distance of the personnel office from the operating agencies. Indeed, many managers view the central personnel office as an outside force and not as a support service. The personnel office also tends to deal with the individual problems in any given unit and does not provide an overall management perspective either for itself or the unit. In other words, it does not have an integrated approach to personnel affairs.

Under a decentralized system, each department has its own personnel officer and staff. The personnel activities are likely to be largely autonomous, and policies and procedures are not uniform. But when each department is permitted to adapt policies and actions to its own needs, the personnel function tends to be closer to the management of the department. The principal problems of the departmental personnel office model are the lack of uniformity among departments, the cost of duplicating the activities in numerous agencies, fewer opportunities for specialization, and the absence of objectivity in handling personnel problems. In most large jurisdictions, the extremes represented by the central and departmental systems are ameliorated by combining them. The central office has certain responsibilities and officials in each department are responsible for the daily personnel activities. Thus the central office can focus on policy development, specialized expertise, monitoring, and review, and the departmental office can concentrate on carrying out the policy in the relevant setting. The departmental office can ask the central office specialist for help when needed. But obviously, not all governmental jurisdictions are large enough to be able to support a specialized personnel office or staff. In such cases, the chief executive officer may very well perform personnel activities along with other duties.

In recent years, the personnel function has spawned a host of new agencies dealing with its particular aspects. Collective bargaining developments have led to the creation of numerous special agencies such as the Federal Labor Relations Authority (FLRA) at the national level and the Public Employee Relations Boards (PERBs) at the state and local levels (for example, Los Angeles, Minnesota, and Maine). Similarly, equal employment opportunity and affirmative action have produced agencies in most jurisdictions to administer those policies. Training and development are yet other functions often found in separately created units. Although these activities may take place outside the personnel office, they are still personnel functions and will be examined later in this book.

Career Systems

Different types of systems operate within the varied personnel structures. Certainly, political appointees and career civil servants represent two different systems interacting within organizations. Technically, the political appointees oversee the career service. During the early part of every new administration, the top-level political appointees promise major shake-ups in the career bureaucracy, but usually nothing changes. The career bureaucrats provide the information and support needed for the programs desired by the agency or department head appointed by the administration, and in most departments, the top administrator cannot risk the career servant's opposition. Accommodations are made, and usually the administrator follows the career servant's recommendations. When this does not happen, career servants lobby for their positions before sympathetic legislative committees.[8]

The political executive's career pattern differs from that of the career service executive, in that the former's tenure in a position depends on the election process.[9] If a new party wins the presidency, governorship, or mayoralty, the political appointees normally will change. And even if a party or administration is reelected, there are likely to be changes in emphasis and thus changes in personnel. Loyalty to the current administration and its policy position is also obligatory for political executives, and dismissal for disagreement is common.

Even more difficult for political executives is that they may have the confidence of the chief executive but become a liability because of political considerations. James Watt, secretary of interior in the Reagan administration, found himself in such a situation. He was Reagan's foil in his attempts to implement controversial decisions involving environmental concerns. But even though Watt was in charge of policy development, he was not wholly responsible for the policy's direction. As an outspoken advocate of the president's policy positions, he was a major target of criticism by the opposition. By taking the heat off Reagan and eventually resigning, Watt aided the president by partially mollifying those who disagreed with the administration's policy. Of course, top political executives usually have no difficulty in finding alternative work and may fade into the background for a short while only to reappear in a new administration. William Ruckelshaus is a good example, having been administrator of the Environmental Protection Agency during the Nixon administration. When President Reagan had to replace another controversial administrator, Anne Burford, Ruckelshaus was called back to put the agency back on a steady course. Interestingly enough, Burford was appointed to a nonpaying position as head of a national advisory committee on the environment little more than a year after she resigned under great pressure as director of the Environmental Protection Agency. Thus, leaving a high-level position in disgrace does not preclude coming back. It is thus very common to see people from previous administrations reappear later in high-level posts, especially under administrations of the same political party.

Career civil servants, of course, have much better tenure prospects and thus carry over from one administration to another. Within that career system, however, are what are referred to as open and closed career systems. Closed career systems are those whose high-level positions are filled entirely through promotion from below. To become a high-level official within the organization, a person must begin at the bottom and advance up through the hierarchical ladder. The military, FBI, Foreign Service, police and fire departments, and the British civil service use such systems. The military is the strictest, but with some exceptions, the others usually require experience at the lower level to attain higher ranks.

An open system means that positions are filled through competition from both inside and outside the organization. Sometimes called lateral entry, the open system allows employees to enter an organization at any level. Open systems are supposed to make the organization more dynamic by bringing in people with fresh ideas and approaches and thus eliminating the stagnation often created by the socialization process within the organization. But in actual practice, most systems that are technically open—as is the case in most government jurisdictions—usually lean more toward the closed system approach. Closed systems are often preferred by employees and employee organizations, as many collective bargaining agreements call for promotion based on seniority, which is a closed system approach. High-level managers often feel more comfortable with a closed system, in that it allows them to deal with known quantities when selecting their staff. People from below can be chosen according to how well they get along and go along in the organization, whereas someone from outside the organization is an unknown quantity.

Closed systems also usually include an up-or-out feature. Up-or-out, or selection-out, refers to the situation in which a person is expected to qualify for promotion within a certain period of time. If he or she is not promoted, the person is dismissed from the organization. The military and Foreign Service use this process, and academic departments in most colleges and universities employ a less strict version of it.

Another element in the career service is the Senior Executive Service (SES). Although the national government's SES, as created by the Civil Service Reform Act of 1978, is the most visible, several states actually preceded the national government in experimenting with the concept. At present, nine states utilize some form of Senior Executive Service.[10] The basic premise of SES is to permit flexibility in using the talents of high-ranking administrators. The objectives of such programs are to:

1. Offer managers opportunities to use talented administrators where they can contribute the most.
2. Offer talented administrators opportunities to broaden their perspectives through wider experiences.
3. Improve communication across organizational units.
4. Improve the image of the public service and thus make easier the recruitment and retention of competent administrators.
5. Improve administrators' performance by rewarding them for outstanding performance.

The success of SES is still questionable. Although the evaluative studies of the national experiment have been fairly negative, the concept itself is still attractive.[11] There is very little evaluative evidence from the state level at this point, but some state experiments have been in existence since 1963 and continue to operate, suggesting that policymakers consider them helpful.

Another variation of the career system is the rank-in-person versus the rank-in-job approach. Rank-in-person means basically that the individual is evaluated and ranked according to his or her performance and compensation and that other benefits are based on the person's rank, regardless of duties performed. Qualifications such as education and experience also help determine the rank. In rank-in-job systems, the position determines the rank and hence the emoluments. Military organizations and, to a certain extent, academic faculties use rank-in-person systems, and most civil service systems are based on rank-in-job. The SES is yet another variation of rank-in-person.

The rank-in-job system and the closed system often produce problems in dealing with good employees, because the only way to advance in salary and prestige and to acquire other badges of success is to travel up through the hierarchy. People are thus rewarded for effective service by promotion to supervisory and managerial positions. These jobs, however, require different skills, and often those good at doing the organization's tasks are not good at managing or supervising others. As a result, some people have suggested a dual or multitrack career system that would permit rewarding individuals for good technical performance while also providing for promotion within the managerial ranks for those with management skills.

The federal Internal Revenue Service has developed—but never implemented—a dual-track system that permits technical employees to attain the same grades in the general schedule as do managerial employees.[12] But again, people who are very good at performing the specialized task in their unit may have difficulty accepting the responsibilities of supervising others. And the way that most of our bureaucracies are currently set up, the only way a person can move up the hierarchy is to become a supervisor or manager. For those who do not have supervisory skills or are not interested in supervisory responsibilities, there is little opportunity for advancement. A dual or multitrack system, therefore, would allow people to move up parallel ladders.[13] One would include supervisory and managerial responsibilities, and the other would recognize greater technical proficiency. Thus, the valuable employee with no interest or skill in supervision would not be placed in such a situation, and the organization would benefit by having only those with such skills in positions to manage other people. To this point, dual or multitrack approaches have not caught on to a great extent in the public service, but they may be one way to alleviate the problems created by the pressures for promotion common in our society.

Intergovernmental Personnel Issues

One of the most significant factors affecting the development of state and local government personnel systems was the variety of federal government requirements imposed on jurisdictions receiving federal grants in aid. Stemming from the Social Security Act of 1939 through the proliferation of categorical grant-in-aid programs during the 1950s, 1960s, and 1970s, state and local governments were prodded to use merit principles for programs funded by federal monies. These federal government requirements were often highly criticized by state and local political officials, who considered them onerous and costly, but they have also been credited with improving many personnel systems across the country.[14] At present, thirty-six states have comprehensive statewide systems, many of which are the direct result of the federal government's requirements. Twenty-four of them were developed after 1939. In 1981, the Reagan administration succeeded in ending federal government personnel conditions associated with grants. Of course, many states impose conditions on their local governments, and many of the federal government's requirements have become institutionalized at the state and local levels. Nonetheless, there is no longer the necessity of maintaining such personnel policies, and there are bound to be changes.

As noted in Chapter 2, general federal governmental policies associated with equal employment opportunity, work safety, and the like still apply to state and local governments. Thus, it is still necessary to be concerned with intergovernmental personnel requirements.

Summary

The personnel function requires that jurisdictions develop structures appropriate to their needs and resources. Systems vary according to the personnel function's intent. Thus, in organizing personnel activities, governments must consider whether they wish to base the system on merit, patronage, or some social purpose. Questions about who should have the authority for personnel activities also must be addressed. In the main, the jurisdiction must develop that structure and those policies that best keep the system responsive to the public, while finding and using the best talent available. All of these concerns depend on resource limitations.

NOTES

1. For background material, see Elmer B. Statts, "Personnel Management: The Starting Place," *Public Personnel Management,* 5 (November-December 1976), 434–441.
2. Muriel M. Morse, "We've Come a Long Way," *Public Personnel Management,* 5 (July-August 1976), 218–224.
3. John Nalbandian, "From Compliance to Consultation: The Changing Role of the Public Personnel Administrator," *Review of Public Personnel Administration,* 1 (Spring 1981), 37–51.
4. See Dennis L. Dresang, "Diffusion of Civil Service Reform: The Federal and State Governments," *Review of Public Personnel Administration,* 2 (Spring 1982), 35–47.
5. Fritz Morstein-Marx, *The Administrative State* (Chicago: University of Chicago Press, 1957), pp. 54–72.
6. Muriel Morse, in a presentation to the Center for Public Service, Texas Tech University, April 18, 1979.
7. Donald E. Klingner, "Political Influences on the Design of State and Local Personnel Systems," *Review of Public Personnel Administration,* 3 (Summer 1981), 1–10.
8. For an interesting commentary on the process, see Leonard Reed, "The Bureaucracy: The Cleverest Lobby of Them All," *Washington Monthly,* 10 (April 1978), 49–54.

9. For an elaboration on the career patterns of political executives, see Dean Mann, "The Selection of Federal Political Executives," *American Political Science Review*, 58 (March 1964), 81–99; and John W. Macy, Bruce Adams, and J. Jackson Walter, *America's Unelected Government* (Cambridge, Mass.: Ballinger, 1983).

10. H. O. Waldby and Annie Mary Hartsfield, "The Senior Management Service in the United States," *Review of Public Personnel Administration*, 4 (Spring 1984), 28–39.

11. For examples of some evaluations, see Michael A. Pagano, "The SES Performance Management System and Bonus Awards," *Review of Public Personnel Administration*, 4 (Spring 1984), 40–56; and Peter W. Colby and Patricia W. Ingraham, "Civil Service Reform: The Views of the Senior Executive Service," *Review of Public Personnel Administration*, 1 (Summer 1981), 75–89.

12. For a good explanation of the IRS system, see Carl L. Bellas, "The Dual Track Career System Within the Internal Revenue Service," *Personnel Administration and Public Personnel Review*, 1 (September-October 1972), 4–8.

13. Russ Smith and Margret Waldie, "Multi-Track Career Ladders: Maximizing Opportunities," *Review of Public Personnel Administration*, 3 (Spring 1983), 15–28.

14. Lawrence D. Greene, "Federal Merit Requirements: A Retrospective Look," *Public Personnel Management*, 11 (Summer 1982), 39–54.

SUGGESTED READINGS

Buchanan, Bruce. "The Senior Executive Service: How We Can Tell If It Works." *Public Administration Review*, 41 (May-June 1981), 349–358.

Colby, Peter W., and Patricia W. Ingraham. "Individual Motivation and Institutional Changes Under the Senior Executive Service." *Review of Public Personnel Administration*, 2 (Spring 1982), 101–118.

Dresang, Dennis L. "Diffusion of Civil Service Reform: The Federal and State Governments." *Review of Public Personnel Administration*, 2 (Spring 1982), 35–47.

Greene, Lawrence D. "Federal Merit Requirements: A Retrospective Look." *Public Personnel Management*, 11 (Summer 1982), 39–54.

Huddleston, Mark W. "Foreign Systems, Familiar Refrains: Civil Service Reform in Comparative Perspective." *Review of Public Personnel Administration*, 2 (Spring 1982), 49–58.

Long, Norton E. "The S.E.S. and the Public Interest." *Public Administration Review*, 41 (May-June 1981), 305–312.

Lynn, Naomi B. "The Civil Service Reform Act of 1978." In Steven W. Hays and Richard C. Kearney, eds., *Public Personnel Administration: Problems and Prospects*. Englewood Cliffs, N.J.: Prentice-Hall, 1983, pp. 347–357.

Macy, John W., Bruce Adams, and J. Jackson Walter. *America's Unelected Government: Appointing the President's Team*. Cambridge, Mass.: Ballinger, 1983.

McGregor, Eugene B., Jr., ed. "Symposium: The Public Service as Institution." *Public Administration Review*, 42 (July-August 1982), 304–320.

Nalbandian, John, and Donald Klingner. "The Politics of Public Personnel Administration: Toward Theoretical Understanding." *"Public Administration Review*, 41 (September-October 1981), 541–549.

Rosen, Bernard. "Uncertainty in the Senior Executive Service." *Public Administration Review*, 41 (March-April 1981), 203–207.

Shapek, Raymond A. "Federal Influences in State and Local Personnel Management: The System in Transition." *Public Personnel Management*, 5 (January-February 1976), 41–51.

Vogelsang-Coombs, Vera, and Marvin Cummins. "Reorganizations and Reforms: Promises, Promises." *Review of Public Personnel Administration*, 2 (Spring 1982), 21–34.

Case 3.1: West Hollywood

In 1984, West Hollywood voters decided to incorporate their own city. The new city is very heavily populated by gays who were at the forefront of the incorporation drive. As the new government is formed, it has become clear that a lot of work must be done to organize the system. Because you are a nationally known expert on personnel management, you are asked to draft recommendations for a personnel system. The system is to be consistent with the state constitution and state law, which require equal employment opportunity and give public employees the right to engage in collective bargaining. Your instructions from the new city council also indicate that a merit system is desired.

INSTRUCTIONS:

Draft your recommendations to the city council, and (1) include a basic personnel policy statement, (2) describe the system's structure, (3) justify your recommendations, and (4) assume that the system works as a weak mayor system of government.

Case 3.2: Instituting Change

The inauguration of Governor Wellerson was an exciting event for Jeff East, the new governor's chief of staff. Having been the campaign manager for Wellerson in an uphill election campaign was the thrill of a lifetime. Now it was time to get to work in carrying out the new governor's promises. Among the major themes of the Wellerson campaign was the view that the public bureaucracy had become too big and too concerned about its own welfare rather than the public's problems. Wellerson promised to bring about a change and to root out all the "incompetent lazy bureaucrats feeding at the public trough." East knew that the electorate had responded positively to that theme, but he also knew that it was rhetoric. He was well aware of the dedication of most public servants and that it would be difficult to accomplish much without their support. He was thus worried that the campaign had created a great deal of distrust of the new governor by the very bureaucracy that would be needed to get things done.

Because of the concerns that East has about being able to work with the public service, which is covered under the state's comprehensive civil service system, he hires you as a consultant to help him devise a means of working with the bureaucracy and to have the governor's program carried out efficiently.

INSTRUCTIONS:

What advice do you give East about how to proceed? How do you gain the trust of the public service? What is the best way of implementing the new governor's program?

4

Instruments of Public Personnel Administration

Various instruments, procedures, and techniques are used to carry out personnel functions. These activities comprise the bulk of traditional personnel management and remain important components of public personnel administration. Among the instruments of personnel management are classification, compensation, recruitment, selection, evaluation, promotion, and discipline. Newer concerns include work-force planning, reductions-in-force (RIFs), training and development, benefits management, and special issues such as job sharing, dual-career couples, and counseling or employee assistance programs. This and the following chapter will briefly review the contributions and limitations of each of the instruments, procedures, and techiques.

Classification

Position classification is a cornerstone of the traditional approach to personnel management and is still the basis on which most public personnel systems are built. In their efforts to make the system fair and just, civil service advocates needed to be able to compare all jobs in the organization. Position classification provides that mechanism and helps managers determine the pay level of any position according to its relative importance. The process describes the duties and responsibilities of each position in the organization and groups the positions into classes according to their similarities for personnel administration purposes.

The classification system's main objective is to permit management to make the most rational decisions regarding the relationship of duties and responsibilities to the other concerns of personnel administration. For instance, a fair compensation plan requires understanding the demands of each position; effective examination and recruiting require knowing what the agency is examining and recruiting for; and determining the qualifications necessary for performing the job requires understanding what the job entails. Position classification evolved as a convenient and useful tool and as an extension of the Scientific Management School's focus on efficiency and economy; it offered a rational approach to organizing activities in a hierarchy, resulting in efficient coordination.

The reaction to spoils and the creation of the Civil Service Commission in 1883 aided the development of position classification, as it offered a means of making personnel decisions according to objective considerations rather than personal and political factors. In order for the Civil Service Commission to establish practical examinations, it needed to have some idea of position duties and responsibilities. In addition, the chaotic federal pay system of the late nineteenth and early twentieth centuries led to pressure for reform. In democratic societies, equal pay for equal work is a readily accepted slogan, at least in the abstract. To apply the principle, positions must be evaluated and classified to give a basis for comparison. Thus the movement toward comprehensive position classification was created from the desire for equality and was reinforced by the increasing complexity of technology and specialization. That it also facilitated management's task in managing positions and people enhanced its appeal.

Position classification originated in the United States and is used more extensively in this country than in other nations. Partly as a response to the good government movements and partly from a concern for fairness and equity, the city of Chicago created position classification, and many state and local governments followed suit.[1] The national government initiated position classification in the federal service with passage of the Classification Act of 1923. The Civil Service Commission acquired responsibility for the process in 1932, and the Classification Act of 1949 authorized the delegation of responsibility for classification to operating departments and agencies. The commission (now the Office of Personnel Management) retained monitoring authority in order to ensure uniformity in the process.

The basic element of the position classification system is the position description. A job must be described in terms of its duties, responsibilities, complexity, working conditions, and skills requirements. These elements are called job factors and vary by jurisdiction but represent the basic job factors that go into any job description. In traditional position classification systems—variously called whole job ranking or grade description—positions are described according to the degree to which each factor is present. The rankings are then determined on the basis of differences among positions. The rankings may be made by a panel of classifiers or by a classification specialist in the personnel agency or operating department. Grades and classes are established to differentiate positions within similar groupings of positions. For example, clericals represent a class of positions and Clerical I, Clerical II, and so on represent grades within a class.

A more recent method of differentiating positions relies on quantification. The same job factors may be used but in the point system and factor comparison approaches, points are assigned to each factor in each job description. Then the points may be weighted for each factor, and the points for all factors are added together. The total points represent the point or factor comparison for the position. The points may be used to distinguish among positions within a class or throughout the organization as a whole. The point factor comparison method is attractive to those who believe that quantification reduces subjectivity. The problem, of course, is that subjectivity is only transferred. Now the subjectivity rests in the points assigned to each factor rather than in the decision about relative place of the whole position in the organizational hierarchy. Nonetheless, using panels for rating factors helps validate the ranking system.

In order to rank the positions, regardless of which system is used, it is necessary to have accurate descriptions of the positions. Three methods are commonly used for describing positions: the employee may be observed performing the position's duties and responsibilities; the employee may be asked to describe the job's duties and responsibilities; or the supervisor may be asked to describe the subordinate's job. In reality, all three approaches are likely to be used in any given jurisdiction.

Usually, the employee is asked to describe the job, and the supervisor then reviews the description and adds comments. If necessary, the classification specialist will then observe the employee in the position. Such observation is common when the reclassification of a position is requested. Having the employee involved is important, in that he or she is likely to know the job best. The employee, however, may sometimes think that particular activities are unimportant. Thus, the supervisor can correct any such oversight and provide perspective on the importance of various tasks. But relying solely on the supervisor is also risky in that the supervisor may not be aware of all the activities and may not realize the extent to which some activities dominate the job. Direct observation also has many other limitations. In particular, the employee may be influenced by the presence of the classification officer and perform differently from normal. Additionally, no one employee is likely to perform all the duties and responsibilities of a position during any short time period. Thus, it is impossible to portray a job accurately only through observation for a short period of time. Some combination of the three approaches thus capitalizes on their strengths and reduces their negative consequences.

Once the job is inventoried through the approaches noted above, it must be described. The job description is supposed to reflect the duties and responsibilities actually performed: it is important that the description portray the job as it really is rather than as the employee or supervisor would like it to be.

Following the description of the position is its classification. Jobs are grouped into classes requiring similar duties, responsibilities, and knowledge, skills, and abilities. The position classification plan is formed by comparing the classes with one another. Just as in describing and grouping positions, there is a lot of room for judgment in ranking the classes, and complete agreement is not likely. However, with the quantitative techniques for factor comparison now being widely used, efforts are being made to reduce the importance of individual judgment.

Clearly it is important that the operating agency or department be closely involved in the classification process, as it knows its unit's tasks best. But, it is also necessary to monitor the classification process to see that there are no abuses, especially overclassification.[2] For example, classification may be used to inflate the importance of a position or unit to the organization. Supervisors and managers gain status according to the number and level of the positions they supervise. Thus, they have an incentive to upgrade the classification of their subordinates' positions in order to inflate the importance of the unit and the supervisor's job. Another problem is that people often become locked into a level of pay, and the only way to increase their pay is to upgrade their position. Although the position classification system is not supposed to be used for this purpose, frustrated managers often see no other way of rewarding good and loyal employees.

Regardless of the reasons for overclassification, the problem does require some form of remedial action. Central personnel offices generally monitor the classification process. In most cases, the positions may be reviewed at any time, but most audits are done in response to an agency's or employee's request. Most personnel systems also use a periodic review. The most common approach is to review each agency's classification plan at regular intervals, but some systems review occupation groups across all agencies. Reviewing a complete plan aids in comparing the different positions within an agency, and reviewing similar positions across departments helps standardize classes of positions. In the latter system, the importance of any particular type of position may be exaggerated as it is the focus of evaluation, and the relationship to other positions is often neglected.

Monitoring position classification places personnel administrators in a difficult spot. The internal political considerations of agency behavior and the concerns of the individual employee make downgrading a classification particularly problematic.[3] Monitors who attempt to lower a classification are viewed as indifferent to the individual's welfare and as a threat to the agency manager's ability to control his or her operation. Moreover, the employee's union or association is likely to get involved as well. Given the alignment of opposition to downgrading classifications, it is no surprise that classification auditors tread lightly.

Position classification comes under attack from many quarters and often represents the policing role that personnel agencies are perceived to play. Managers of operating departments often see the classification process as one that inhibits them. Their attention to classification as an end in itself rather than to how it can support management leads to opposition to it.

A recent attempt at dealing with the problems of classification is the average grade approach. In such a system, all positions in an organization are assigned points according to their class, grade, and salary level.[4] The sum of points for all positions in the organization then becomes a base for the organization. When an employee leaves a position, the points assigned to that position may be reallocated among other positions in the unit. Thus, for a Keypunch Operator I, three points may be assigned, a Keypunch Operator II receives seven points, and a Keypunch Operator III receives ten points. If a Keypunch Operator III resigns, the unit will have ten points to redistribute. There are several possibilities for the redistribution. A new Keypunch Operator I and a new Keypunch Operator II may be hired. Or the Keypunch Operator II may be promoted a grade using three of the points, and then another II appointed to use the remaining seven points. Of course, the department manager will have other positions with other point values in the organization and may redistribute the points among them. The point is that the manager has some flexibility to recognize the employees' contributions and to use the points to reward them and to realign positions within the organization to adapt to its changing needs.

An alternative to position classification is to differentiate jobs on the basis of the incumbent employee. Such an approach is referred to as rank-in-person. It uses the individual employee's abilities, credentials, and experience as the basis for making personnel decisions, particularly deciding on compensation. Personnel decisions in this approach are more subjective than are those in the rank-in-job system. Moreover, subordinates find it difficult to accept comparisons with other employees when they cannot see the whole picture. The criteria for making decisions are much less clear than in the position classification approach, and thus most managers worry more because they have to justify their decisions and do not have objective criteria for taking action.

Rank-in-person systems appear to be most appropriate for professional personnel who are accustomed to being evaluated on the basis of their experience, education, and other credentials. But even so, ranking such people is not easy.

In reality, the position classification and rank-in-person approaches tend to be combined. It is almost impossible to conceive of a position classification system in which the incumbent does not influence the classification. Some of the abuses of the system, such as overclassification, result from supervisors' consideration of the needs and qualities of the incumbent in the position. Each employee brings different capabilities to the position, and each may expand or contract its scope of duties and responsibilities. The average grade approach, discussed above, is an example of intentionally mixing the two systems.

The current concern for meaningful employment situations and individual liberty will continue to affect personnel, but position classification is likely to retain its hold on most public personnel activities. Most bureaucracies are still organized according to the traditional hierarchy, and position classification is a natural complement to that form of organization. Personnel administrators and departmental managers are likely to resist innovations that use less convenient criteria for making personnel decisions.

Position Management

Jay Shafritz conceptualized the personnel process as one of position management in which work is analyzed according to the organization's mission and jobs are designed so as to maximize the effectiveness of an agency's human resources.[5] The concept of position management incorporates features of rank-in-job and rank-in-person by recognizing that many factors affect the productivity of employees and organizations.

JOB DESIGN

Closely associated with position classification is job design. Job design refers to the way a position is structured, including what duties and responsibilities it involves. Position classification often creates narrowly defined jobs that become extremely boring. Effective job design can eliminate such problems by making the job challenging and giving the employee as much discretion as possible. Recognizing that behavioral concerns, such as the employees' needs, motivation, and environment, are as important to job performance as are assigned duties, position management attempts to incorporate these concerns in the way that work is organized and distributed.

Consider an office responsible for monitoring the receipt of sales tax monies. If one position deals only with receiving monies, another with recording receipts, a third with checking records, and a fourth with follow-up investigations, employees are likely to become bored with their repetitive tasks. If, however, they are assigned to particular accounts and are responsible for all the activities associated with them, they are likely to find the jobs more interesting and challenging.

QUALIFICATION REQUIREMENTS

A direct result of the classification and job design processes is the development of qualification standards. These are the qualities that an individual must possess to perform the duties and meet the responsibilities of a given position. Because qualification standards are pertinent to the recruitment process, they will be discussed more fully with that topic.

Compensation

Compensation is the financial reward that individuals receive for their work in the organization. It may be direct salary and wages or a benefit such as vacation, sick leave, retirement pension, and health insurance. In the public sector, compensation is always a major issue because the taxpayers naturally want to make sure that their tax money is not wasted. Public employees' salaries represent a major expense to the taxpayers and are easy targets when citizens become upset with some government activity. Similarly, managers are concerned with pay, in that it affects their ability to influence activity in the organization through the distribution of rewards. Employees are concerned for obvious reasons. Pay therefore becomes a sensitive issue if any one of these groups perceives it to be unfairly distributed. The employees' morale, in particular, is affected to the extent that they may feel that their salary is or is not equitable and appropriate.

In systems with formal classification plans, a compensation plan is a natural complement. The compensation plan is constructed from the differences established in grouping positions by class and grade. The pay plan normally establishes a pay rate according to the position's classification, and the classification and compensation plans are closely related. Because of controversy over how different jobs are valued, the traditional compensation plan has been under attack.[6]

In determining pay, public managers must now consider such issues as merit, pay for performance, comparability pay, collective bargaining, equity, comparable worth, and benefits. In addition, methods of establishing the pay scale and resolving conflicts and grievances occupy the time of public personnel administrators.

As with all other features of the personnel system, the jurisdiction's basic policy normally establishes some guidelines for compensation. For example, legislatures are usually given the authority to set compensation. But because legislatures are often pressed for time and prefer not to get into the details of pay scales, they usually delegate the authority to someone else, normally the civil service board or personnel agency. Thus, executive branches commonly are responsible for drawing up a compensation plan and make recommendations to the legislative body for its final adoption. Of course, in those state and local governments that bargain over pay, compensation levels are established through negotiation between management and employee union representatives.

Political leaders and citizens often focus on the costs of public personnel. Because personnel costs typically make up at least half of government's expenditures, it is easy to single out the public bureaucrat as the culprit in government cost. Given the image of the public bureaucracy, taxpayers are easily led by politicians who rail against the "bloated bureaucracy." In the past, public employees were perceived as underpaid compared with their counterparts in the private sector. Now, however, many public employees seem to fare quite well compared with others. Although top-level managers in the public sector, especially the federal government, usually lag far behind their private sector counterparts, people in the middle and lower levels often do better than comparable employees in the private sector. There is great variation in the state and local bureaucracies, with many jurisdictions still trailing the private sector, whereas others, especially large jurisdictions, may pay their employees comparatively well.

Several factors have contributed to the changes in the status of public employees. Collective bargaining, which came to the public sector mostly during the 1960s and 1970s, helped greatly in closing the gap between public and private sector employees. Comparability pay, in which public employees' salaries are based on the findings of comparative studies of similar positions in other jurisdictions or the private sector, is a policy that has been adopted by many governments, including the federal government. Comparability pay has led to greater equity between the public and private sectors. The benefits for lower- and middle-level public employees in large jurisdictions have generally been better than for their private sector counterparts, although private sector top-level managers normally have many more benefits and perquisites than do comparable employees in the public sector. In the past, comparability studies excluded benefits from the comparability formula. By focusing only on salary and wages, public employees have generally improved their status relative to that of private sector employees, because their salaries have become comparable and their better benefit packages have remained. But these inequities have been disappearing in recent years, as governments commonly now include benefits as part of the comparability considerations. Such systems are referred to as total compensation comparability packages. Comparability pay is also criticized because it opens the door to never-ending increases in compensation costs.

Another controversial aspect of public sector compensation is the relationship between cost-of-living adjustments and adjustments based on merit or performance. The merit pay controversy in education and pay for performance elements of the Civil Service Reform Act of 1978 and state and local reforms are representative of the issue.[7] Although it is difficult to find people opposed to the concept of paying on the basis of merit, there are serious reservations concerning who is to define merit, what criteria are to be used, and how the merit money is to be distributed. Employees, and especially employee unions, are concerned that if management determines the criteria and decides who will receive merit pay, the abuse of discretion is likely to lead to favoritism and inequity. More importantly, definitions of merit are not always shared. Employees' legitimate concerns often become politicized, as happened when President Reagan and public school teachers quarreled over merit pay for teachers. The issues got lost in the rhetoric. When policies state that only half the employees (or fewer) in any unit may receive merit increases, inequities are inevitable. A unit with all very productive employees would be penalized, as only a portion of the employees could receive merit increases, whereas others in an unproductive unit could qualify for such increases. Obviously, the inequities result from the policy and not the concept itself. But the mechanisms for implementing merit pay have contributed to the problems and the resistance to it by many employees. At the same time, there are arguments that employees who provide satisfactory, although not outstanding performance, should not be penalized by inflation which reduces the real value of their incomes. Thus, pay packages usually offer some combination of cost of living and merit pay.

Another recent controversial issue is comparable worth. Comparable worth refers to equal pay for work of comparable value. The problem is that personnel systems have determined the value of particular work through job evaluation systems that have incorporated discriminatory criteria. As a result, classes of positions that are dominated by women or minorities are usually valued at a lower pay rate than are those dominated by white males. For the past two decades, the median salary of women has hovered around 60 percent of the median salary of men. In recent years, pressure has been brought to bear on personnel systems to rectify discriminatory practices through legislative efforts, litigation, and collective bargaining negotiations.[8] The issue promises to continue to be controversial and will be examined in greater detail in Chapter 8.

Work-Force Planning

Work-force planning would seem to be an important element of the public personnel function, in that it requires assessing the employer's future needs and strategies for ensuring that such needs will be met. Thus, work-force planning requires understanding what skills are needed in the jurisdiction's employees and deciding whether the labor market is able to supply those needs. In the absence of skills in the labor force and market, it is necessary to develop strategies for training the employees already in the organization. Thus, work-force planning also means devising effective means of improving the skills of current employees and offering them promotional opportunities.

Though the need for planning seems obvious, public managers often find it difficult to do much. Of course, political and other considerations may constrain the amount of planning that can be done. Sudden shifts in political values or priorities can also destroy plans. During the 1960s and early 1970s, for example, government employment increased dramatically, especially at the state and local levels. As a result, expectations were that there would be a continued growth and need for more employees. Most jurisdictions, therefore, were unprepared for the radical change that came with the tax revolts and the passage of tax reduction and limitation laws, inspired by Proposition 13 in California in 1978. With financial resources suddenly and drastically reduced, governments had to start planning on how to reduce payrolls rather than increasing them.

Work-force planning is usually not a priority for public managers when they have to face the daily demands of citizens and others interested in their activities. Indeed, planning of any kind in government is often difficult because of the politically elected officials' lack of stability in tenure: when elected leaders change, so do many of the system's priorities. Thus, plans can become obsolete very quickly. Governments' recent cutback programs have not produced any significant evidence that planning is any greater a part of public personnel management than before.[9] Clearly, planning could be a significant aspect of all public personnel management activities, but there are very few constituencies urging public managers to do much planning.

Staffing

Staffing public agencies requires methods for recruiting, examining, selecting, and promoting people so that the organization can get its work done.

RECRUITMENT

Recruitment is the process whereby an employer seeks qualified applicants for vacant or potentially vacant positions. In times of high unemployment, such as in the late 1970s into the mid-1980s, attracting a large pool of qualified applicants poses no problems. During low unemployment times, however, government has to compete with private industry, and given the image of the public service, it is not always easy for government to recruit. Government employees also take a lot of abuse from elected officials, the media, and the general public. As a result, many qualified people would rather work for private industry, in which they are more insulated from such pressures. Nonetheless, there are many people who prefer the excitement of the public spotlight and politics or who just have a strong commitment to public service. Thus, there are people in government service as highly qualified as those in industry. The problem is in continuing to attract highly qualified people.

During the 1970s, governments found themselves under different pressures in the recruitment process. With passage of the Equal Employment Opportunity Act of 1972, state and local governments became subject to antidiscrimination legislation. As a result, efforts had to be made to recruit women and minorities for all types of positions in government. Charges of discrimination could be brought against a jurisdiction by anyone who felt discriminated against in the personnel process. If the jurisdiction were found to be discriminatory in its practices, it could be required to make restitution to the individual(s) directly discriminated against and was usually forced to develop a plan to eliminate discrimination in the future. Many federal grants contained conditions according to which they could be revoked if the jurisdiction did not follow equal employment opportunity policies.

Affirmative action is a process by which an employer makes positive efforts to recruit those people who have been discriminated against in the past. Affirmative action plans became common parts of personnel policies across the country, as federal agencies often required them in order to be eligible for many grants and as monitoring agencies and courts ordered the development of such plans to reverse past discriminatory practices. But the Reagan administration has deemphasized affirmative action and equal opportunity and the current Supreme Court seems to be retreating on the issue, as well; thus state and local governments are under less pressure to maintain equal employment opportunity. Advocates of equal opportunity and affirmative action are hopeful, nonetheless, that the concept has attained widespread enough acceptance that jurisdictions will continue such efforts because it is the just and fair thing to do. Even with the enforcement of equal employment opportunity policies, females and minorities have had widely varying degrees of success in state and local governments. They have been employed in increasing numbers, but the types of jobs and levels of positions they have been given suggest continuing patterns of discrimination.[10]

Recruitment processes can be discriminatory in themselves because of the qualifications required for the position or because of the recruitment market. Public employers often exaggerate the credentials necessary for a position because they feel that such requirements will lead to a better quality of employee. Such a justification has other implications, however. It may mean getting an employee who is overqualified and who will not be satisfied with the position. It may also mean that people who could do the job very well are not considered because they do not have the credentials required. Such an effect is often discriminatory because some groups have been systematically denied the opportunity to gain certain credentials, whether they be education or experience. Equal employment opportunity policy prohibits using a qualification requirement unless it can be shown to be relevant to the position.

Some recent efforts to overcome discriminatory recruitment policies have included job sharing and the employment of dual-career couples. Job sharing permits an organization to hire two or more people to do what would ordinarily be done by one. The job sharers work reduced hours and share one position. With such an arrangement, the focus can be on accommodating people's unique scheduling problems (caring for children, for example) or on dividing the position along the lines of skills needed. Thus, if part of the job requires a specific highly developed skill, it is possible that one part-time employee will have that skill and that another, less skilled individual can be employed to fulfill the job's other functions.

Dual-career couples are another important element of the labor market. Often, spouses have difficulty finding employment in their specializations in the same labor market. Such is particularly true in academic institutions. Unless the couple lives in a large urban area, chances are that two academics will have difficulty being employed in the same field or even in different fields. Some employers make adjustments to accommodate the needs of such couples, including job sharing in which the couple shares one position. With two people in one position the organization often is much more productive than it would be with one individual in the position. At the same time, the couple can pursue their professional interests together.

The recruitment process, if successful, results in a number of applicants who meet the minimum standards for a position. The next step is to select which applicant to hire. Selection is based on an assessment of the candidates' qualifications, and in many jurisdictions an examination is used to narrow further the field of applicants.

EXAMINATIONS

Examinations are the mainstays of public sector selection processes. The exam may be either assembled or unassembled. The unassembled exam normally is an evaluation of an applicant's background, experience, and references. The information comes from the application and other documentation required in the application process, along with follow-ups on recommendations and from former employers. These exams are most useful for managerial and professional positions, but many small jurisdictions without extensive resources also use them for most of their positions.

The assembled exam is more commonly employed, particularly at the state and national levels and in large local jurisdictions. Assembled exams are usually written examinations but may also include oral interviews or problem-solving situations. In some cases, assessment center procedures are used, in which applicants are placed in a highly structured situation and engage in some form of simulation exercise.[11] Assembled exams may also require some type of performance test, such as taking shorthand or running a computer program. Many jurisdictions use combinations of any of these types of exam. The written exam is commonly used as a preliminary screening device, and then others may be used as appropriate.

Making sure that the exams test the appropriate skills means making sure that they are valid. There is often a problem with regard to the relevance of general knowledge or aptitude exams, although they are often used. There are three main types of validity—that of content, criterion, and construct.

Content validity means that an exam measures factors directly related to the duties and responsibilities of the position in question. Content validity is particularly useful in positions calling for a definable and measurable skill. For example, the content validity of typing tests for secretarial work is easy to verify.

Criterion validity refers to whether an exam is a good predictor of performance on the job. Thus employees may be selected and then a year later a comparison made between their scores on the entrance exam and on their performance evaluations or other criteria. This is known as criterion validation and entails giving an exam to those already in the positions. If the exam is valid, those who score well on it should be successful employees whose performance is rated high by their supervisors and vice versa.

Construct validity is more difficult to achieve because it applies to tests that measure more elusive qualities, such as ability and flexibility. Construct validation is useful for managerial decision-making positions whose precise job content is difficult to establish.

The validity of examinations has become a major issue in the wake of equal employment opportunity. To make sure that the personnel system is not discriminatory, employers must see that their examination procedures are valid. For if examinations are found to have an adverse impact on minorities and females, they may be invalidated by the courts. Adverse impact means that the members of such groups have a smaller chance of being selected than do others. According to federal guidelines, adverse impact is assumed if the selection rate for a given protected group is less than 80 percent of the rate with the greatest selection success. This selection rate is widely used, but the Supreme Court has demonstrated flexibility, indicating that the overall employment record and the particular content of the employer's actions will be considered when deciding such cases.[12] Although examinations will continue to have to meet the relevance criterion, it does seem that the employer's total personnel system is being given more consideration.

SELECTION

Personnel offices certify applicants to the unit doing the hiring after reviewing their applications and exams. Certification means that the employing unit may choose from among the candidates listed as eligible by the personnel office. In the federal government, and in many other jurisdictions, the rule of three is used, meaning that any of the top three applicants can be selected. Other jurisdictions normally use some variation in the number certified as eligible.

The purpose of certifying more than one name is to give some flexibility to the manager doing the hiring. Because of the exams' fallibility, few people want to rely on them exclusively. Moreover, some people do well on assembled exams but may not fit into the organization satisfactorily. Thus, the manager has the opportunity to make these judgments, but the decision rules also limit that discretion to the top candidates.

The rule of three or other such rules, however, may be unrealistic, as the time elapsed between the administration of the exam and the certification is usually long. The top candidates often have already accepted other job offers, and the agency may be forced to go down the list to find one willing to accept the position. Too, the scores are often separated by very small differences, and differentiating among the candidates on the basis of fractions of points is questionable, especially in jurisdictions in which exams are not regularly validated and updated. One solution is to group the examinees by natural breaking points in the scores and then to select from those above the relevant breaking point. But such suggestions have not been given much weight in the public sector.

Veterans' preference complicates the selection process. Veterans' groups have been effective lobbyists in convincing Congress and state legislators to enact veterans' preference as an easy way to gain political support from an influential group. Traditionally, the federal service gave a bonus of five points to all veterans and a ten-point bonus to disabled veterans who passed the general competitive exam. As the federal service has disbanded its general exam and instructed the individual departments to draw up their own, the regulations now apply to departmentally developed and administered exams. In some jurisdictions, veterans get absolute preference; that is, they go to the top of the list if they receive a minimum passing score. The preference given to veterans may thus interfere with the appointing official's ability to select the best candidate, because the top scorers are pushed aside by veterans who receive bonus points. In most instances, they probably perform ably, but there is always the chance that more capable people are being turned away. The absolute preference system used at some state and local levels and at the entry level in the federal service for disabled veterans represents the most extreme problem. This inequity is also increased in some jurisdictions by giving the same preferences to the spouses and children of veterans.

Although veterans' preference laws have been under strong attack in recent years, little change has been forthcoming. As part of the Civil Service Reform Act of 1978, President Carter attempted to reduce the preference and limit the time during which veterans could claim the preferential treatment. But veterans' groups mobilized their members and mounted an effective counter lobby to the proposal. Ironically, instead of reducing preference, the legislation actually offered additional benefits to veterans with disabilities, allowing them appointments without competitive examination and retention rights during reductions in force. Challenges at the state level have been taken to the courts. Helen Feeney challenged Massachusetts's absolute preference law, which put veterans who pass the exam ahead of everyone else. She had taken the civil service promotion exams three times during the twelve years she was employed by the state. Each time, veterans were put ahead of her becaue of the absolute preference system. By a seven-to-two decision, the court upheld the state statute, noting that the law did not discriminate on the basis of sex, even though veterans are almost always male.[13] Thus any efforts to change such provisions will have to be directed to legislative bodies. The implications for public service go beyond quality, as such preferential treatment remains an obstacle to females and thus to the affirmative action process.

Selection procedures usually provide temporary or emergency appointments when competitive selection would be impossible. Ordinarily such appointments expire within a specified period of time. The time is provided so that examinations and other procedures can be prepared. But if the position itself is a temporary one, competitive exams may not be required by personnel rules. Nonetheless, there is often abuse in using temporary appointments. Employers may use temporary appointments to retain people who might not qualify for a permanent position. Some employers continually reappoint "temporary" employees, renewing the appointments each time they expire. They thus become permanent employees for all intents and purposes. Of course, such employees can easily be intimidated by the threat of not renewing the appointment.

Selection may be made from within the agency, thus excluding from consideration those outside. And frequently, examinations are open only to those inside the organization. Promotion is the common method of filling positions from within and will be discussed later. Selection from within is often favored by employee organizations as a way of assuring employees an opportunity for advancement. Management normally favors outside recruitment to bring in new ideas, but collective bargaining has tended to increase the practice of selection from within.

PROMOTION

Promotion provides an opportunity for employees to advance in the organization. Through promotion, they gain status in the organization and ordinarily improve their salary levels as well. Management also uses promotion as a way of keeping valuable employees and increasing their input into the organization's activities. Ideally, promotions are based on the employee's merit and the organization's needs. As in all decisions in which human beings are involved, however, merit is not always the major consideration. Both management and employee organizations have interests in the process and attempt to structure promotions to serve their interests. From management's perspective, merit is important, but so also is the employee's attitude and ability to work within the organization. Thus, promotion is often used to weed out those who may challenge the organization's values and goals and to reward those who show the "proper" respect for the agency's policies and values.[14] Employee organizations such as unions usually prefer to use seniority as the basis for promotion, as it is something that is easily quantifiable and leaves little to the management's discretion.

Promotions may hamper the organization if they are based on rewarding those who accept the agency's perspective on everything. Because promotions go to those who agree with management, new ideas are unlikely to be introduced to the organization, and the public may suffer because the agency's problems will probably not be resolved and new approaches to providing services not be considered. Protection of the status quo or accretion of more power may become more important aims than providing quality service to the public. To prevent such stagnation in agencies, open competition for positions by people inside and outside the organization can be used.

Except for seniority, the criteria for promotion are difficult to establish. Managers frequently promote an employee who has demonstrated good or outstanding performance in a specific job. Supervisory responsibility, however, requires skills different from those for the work supervised. As a result, employees are often promoted to positions for which they are not skilled. Public sector agencies increasingly recognize the problem of unskilled supervisors and try to resolve it through better selection processes. Assessment centers have become popular methods for evaluating employees' supervisory and managerial potential, but because they are very expensive, their use is limited. A more recent approach is the Objective Judgment Quotient (OJQ), by which employees are rated by selected associates.[15] Because the raters are familiar with the organization and the job, the process is much more organization specific than is the typical assessment center. Using the organization's own employees in the rating process also reduces its costs.

Summary

The traditional instruments for carrying out public personnel functions continue to influence public personnel management. Thus personnel administrators need to develop effective systems for classifying positions, compensating employees, and relating those systems to the organization's work. Public employers also must create ways of recruiting and selecting the best workers possible. To keep those employees it is necessary to have career opportunities for them, thus promotional ladders and systems. All of these functions are performed under increasing pressures to eliminate inequities and offer equal employment opportunities. The next chapter will study more instruments of public personnel management.

NOTES

1. Civil Service Assembly, *Position Classification in the Public Service* (Chicago: Civil Service Assembly, 1941, reprinted in 1965 by the Public Personnel Association, successor of the Civil Service Assembly). Chapter 2 discusses historical development. This book is the most comprehensive analysis available on position classification.

2. Maurice Penner, "How Job-based Classification Systems Promote Organizational Ineffectiveness," *Public Personnel Management*, 12 (Fall 1983), 268–276.

3. For an examination of the issue, see Gilbert A. Schulkind, "Monitoring Position Classification: Practical Problems and Possible Solutions," *Public Personnel Management*, 4 (January-February 1976), 32–37.

4. John F. DeSanto, "Higher Pay for Good Performance—The Average Grade Approach," *Public Personnel Management*, 9 (1980), 282–284.

5. Jay M. Shafritz, *Public Personnel Management: The Heritage of Civil Service Reform* (New York: Praeger, 1975), chap. 4.

6. An excellent discussion of what determines the value of different jobs is presented by Helen Remick, "The Comparable Worth Controversy," *Public Personnel Management* 10 (Winter 1981), 371–383.

7. See Daniel E. O'Toole and John R. Churchill, "Implementing Pay for Performance: Initial Experiences," *Review of Public Personnel Administration*, 3 (Summer 1982), 13–28; and Ed Kitchen, "Greensboro's Performance-based Pay Plan," *Popular Government*, (Summer 1980), 1–5, 16.

8. Good reviews of the issue may be found in Elaine Johansen, "Managing the Revolution: The Case of Comparable Worth," *Review of Public Personnel Adminstration*, 4 (Spring 1984), 14–27; and Steven M. Neuse, "A Critical Perspective on the Comparable Worth Debate," *Review of Public Personnel Administration*, 3 (Fall 1982), 1–20.

9. Arthur T. Johnson, "Cutback Strategies and Public Personnel Management: An Analysis of Nine Maryland Counties," *Review of Public Personnel Administration*, 3 (Fall 1982), 41–55.

10. N. Joseph Cayer and Lee Sigelman, "Minorities and Women in State and Local Government: 1973–1975," *Public Administration Review*, 40 (September-October 1980), 443–450; Nelson C. Dometrius, "Minorities and Women Among State Agency Leaders," *Social Science Quarterly*, 65 (March 1984), 127–137; P. Grabosky and D. Rosenbloom, "Racial and Ethnic Integration in the Federal Service," *Social Science Quarterly*, 56 (June 1975), 71–84; Grace Hall and Alan Saltzstein, "Equal Employment Opportunity for Minorities in Municipal Government," *Social Science Quarterly*, 57 (March 1977), 864–872; Matthew Hutchins and Lee Sigelman, "Black Employment in State and Local Governments: A Comparative Analysis," *Social Science Quarterly*, 62 (March 1981), 79–87; Russell L. Smith, "Representative Bureaucracy: A Research Note on Demographic Representation in State Bureaucracies," *Review of Public Personnel Administration*, 1 (Fall 1980), 1–13; and Susan A. Welch, Albert K. Karnig, and Richard A. Eribes, "Changes in Hispanic Local Public Employment in the Southwest," *Western Political Quarterly*, 36 (December 1983), 660–673, are only a few of the many studies on this issue.

11. For an excellent analysis of what assessment centers are and the abuses associated with them, see Joyce D. Ross, "A Current Review of Public-Sector Assessment Centers: Cause for Concern," *Public Personnel Management*, 8 (January-February 1979), 41–46.

12. See Dee Ann Hortsman, "New Judicial Standards for Adverse Impact: Their Meaning for Personnel Practices," *Public Personnel Management*, 7 (November-December 1978), 347–353, for an in-depth analysis of the Court's position.

13. *Massachusetts* v *Feeney*, 47 LW 4651 (1979).
14. See Charles Perrow, *Organizational Analysis: A Sociological View* (Belmont, Calif.: Brooks/Cole, 1970), pp. 52–54; Anthony Downs, *Inside Bureaucracy* (Boston: Little, Brown, 1967), pp. 228–231, and Robert T. Golembiewski, *Behavior and Organization: O & M and the Small Group* (Chicago: Rand McNally, 1962), pp. 186–190.
15. Mark R. Edwards, "OJQ Offers Alternative to Assessment Center," *Public Personnel Administration*, 12 (Summer 1983), 146–155.

SUGGESTED READINGS

Burrington, Debra D. "Review of State Government Employee Application Forms for Suspect Inquiries," *Public Personnel Management*, 11 (Spring 1982), 55–60.

Davis, Charles E. "Veteran's Preference and Civil Service Employment: Issues and Policy Implications." *Review of Public Personnel Administration*, 3 (Fall 1982), 57–65.

Eisinger, Peter K. *The Politics of Displacement*. New York: Academic Press, 1980.

Epperson, Lawrence L. "The Dynamics of Factor Comparison/Point Evaluation." *Public Personnel Management*, 4 (January-February 1975), 38–48.

Frank, Michael S. "Position Classification: A State-of-the-Art Review and Analysis." *Public Personnel Management*, 11 (Fall 1982), 239–247.

Harvey, Barron H., Jerome F. Rogers, and Judy A. Schultze. "Sick Pay vs. Well Pay: An Analysis of the Impacts of Rewarding Employees for Being on the Job." *Public Personnel Management* 12 (Summer 1983), 218–224.

Johansen, Elaine. "Managing the Revolution: The Case of Comparable Worth." *Review of Public Personnel Administration*, 4 (Spring 1984), 14–27.

Karnig, Albert K., and Susan A. Welch. *Black Representation and Urban Policy*. Chicago: University of Chicago Press, 1980.

Nachmias, David, and Paul J. Moderachi. "Patterns of Support for Merit Pay and EEO Performance: The Inherent Difficulties of Implementing Innovation." *Policy Studies Journal*, 11 (December 1982), 318–327.

Sackett, Paul R. "A Critical Look at Some Common Beliefs About Assessment Centers." *Public Personnel Administration*, 11 (Summer 1982), 140–147.

Smith, Russell L. "Representative Bureaucracy: A Research Note on Demographic Representation in State Bureaucracies." *Review of Public Personnel Administration*, 1 (Fall 1980), 1–13.

Smith, Russ, and Margret Waldie. "Multi-Track Career Ladders: Maximizing Opportunities." *Review of Public Personnel Management*, 3 (Spring 1983), 15–28.

Thompson, Frank, and Bonnie Browne. "Commitment to the Disadvantaged Among Urban Administrators: The Case of Minority Hiring." *Urban Affairs Quarterly*, 13 (March 1978), 355–378.

White, Robert D. "Position Analysis and Characterization." *Review of Public Personnel Administration*, 4 (Spring 1984), 57–67.

Case 4.1: Hiring a Police Chief

The city of Beech Grove is searching for a new chief of police. The previous chief left after just two years in office. It seems that the police department has a bad image problem in the community, and the previous chief did not handle public relations well. In addition, the department has been undergoing some major reorganization because of low morale and productivity. There is a feeling in the department that communication is bad and its personnel do not feel much commitment.

There were seventeen applicants for the position of chief, and the committee has narrowed its list to two, Marie Corley and Joan Galt. Each comes with high recommendations, and you, the city manager, must give your decision to the city council at next week's meeting.

Marie Corley is now a member of the police command staff, having recently been promoted to assistant chief of police. She has been a resident of the city all of her life. She is well known in the community and seems to be a favorite of the local press. Her management skills are less well known, however. Her rise in the ranks of the department was primarily the result of special projects she worked on, especially involving the local citizens in crime prevention programs. But Corley has not actually supervised or managed other employees.

Joan Galt is the assistant chief of police in Garden Shores, a larger community nearby. She worked her way up through the ranks of her department and has held every supervisory job in the ranks. Her reputation is one of an outstanding manager who is well liked by the whole department. She is an unknown quantity outside the department, however. She has not been involved in external relations and thus has had little experience with the general public. But her colleagues and subordinates in her department give her high marks as a leader and manager.

INSTRUCTIONS:

Given this information, what would be your recommendation? Why? Would there be anything else you would be likely to do before making your recommendation?

Case 4.2: The Interview

Helen Wells was excited about having been called in for an interview for a job as the liaison between the city planning department and the city council staff. The job also involved working with community-based groups interested in planning and zoning issues. Her interview was with Harry Jameson, the planning director.

As the interview began, Mr. Jameson made small talk about the terrible weather and how it would be nice when it warmed up a bit. Then he turned to specific questions concerning Helen's potential employment by the city. He asked the following:

1. Why do you think you would be the person we should hire for the job?
2. What skills do you have that would make you effective in performing the job's tasks?
3. What is your political affiliation?
4. When did you graduate from high school? College?
5. Do you have small children?
6. Have you ever been arrested?
7. To what social and professional organizations do you belong?
8. What is the general state of your health?
9. How long have you lived in the city?
10. Are there any questions you would like to ask me?

> After Helen asked a few questions about the planning department and its personnel policy, the interview ended and Helen left. She felt that the interview had gone well and that she had made a good impression. However, she had also been uncomfortable with some of the questions that were asked. She felt that she had to answer them in order to have any chance at the job but also believed that many of them were inappropriate.

INSTRUCTIONS:

1. Was Helen overreacting? Explain.
2. Examine each question and indicate whether or not it is appropriate.

3. Even though a particular question may be inappropriate, is there legitimate information that it was intended to elicit? How might the question be framed to get the legitimate information?

5

Keeping Employees Productive

T he ultimate test of the public service and its personnel system is
its employees' performance. In recent years, performance and
its improvement have been of particular concern to public managers and citizens. Shrinking resources, inflation, and collective bargaining demands all contribute to need for top performance by public
employees. This chapter will examine the role of supervisors, motivation techniques, productivity, performance evaluation, discipline, and
training and development, all of which pertain to securing optimal
performance. We shall also consider cutback management, reduction
in force, and contracting out, as pressures on performance.

The Supervisor

Supervisors are generally considered to be the key to the employees' performance. Although there is some evidence to suggest that
supervision contributes only a small part to the organization's productivity, it is still important to establishing the organization's smooth
operation so that work can be accomplished.[1] Supervisors have a number of tasks related to the performance of those under them. They
must see that the job gets done, keep work areas safe, encourage
teamwork and cooperation, assist in developing employee skills, and
maintain records.[2] Because employees and work situations vary from
agency to agency, the approaches must vary as well. The supervisors
themselves need training in their supervisory tasks if organizations are
to avoid the pitfalls of the Peter Principle, which states that "in a
hierarchy, every employee tends to rise to his level of incompetence."[3]
To perform well as a supervisor thus calls for many kinds of skills.

The supervisor's job requires dealing with a wide variety of needs and types of employees. Some employees are motivated primarily by the money the job pays and work only to earn the resources to enjoy the standard of living they want. Such employees are not motivated by their work and need relatively structured supervision to keep them productive. Others may be more concerned about being in a friendly work place and enjoy the company of others and are motivated by the organization's social norms and congeniality. Still others need to control their own careers and require significant independence to work within the responsibilities of their jobs. These people, assuming they have the ability, can be given responsibility and are likely to respond favorably. Still other employees are motivated by the work itself. They are concerned with whether the work is socially meaningful or contributes to some goal to which they are committed.

In dealing with different employees, supervisors must realize that some employees need detailed instructions and others need a great deal of independence. Some need to be left alone, and others need to be stroked constantly. No two employees will be exactly alike, and so supervisors must use various techniques to motivate performance from different people. Some of the resources needed for motivating employees are available to the supervisor, but others are outside his or her control. Certainly a supervisor can create a friendly, open, and authority-sharing work situation. But the supervisor cannot alone determine monetary rewards, advancement, and the opportunity for controlling the work situation; upper management usually has final say in these matters.

The supervisor's approach will depend on his or her knowledge of the employees and their needs. It will also depend on the technology available and the authority the supervisor has to make changes. In addition, employee unions and organizations increasingly affect management's ability to use performance improvement techniques. Thus the role of the labor organization decides, in part, what will be done in the agency.

Approaches to Motivation

Traditional theorists viewed human beings as primarily rational and motivated by economic considerations. Furthermore, traditional theory based its techniques on the belief that people disliked work and had to be induced to work through economic rewards that would permit them to satisfy their material needs. According to this view, the way to attract employees was to offer them good pay, and the way to increase their productivity was to raise their salaries. In the industrial sector, where productivity was usually more easily measured, the emphasis on material incentives led to the use of piece-rate forms of compensation in which the employee could earn more by producing more. Gradually, theorists learned that money would motivate employees to a certain point, but then it lost value as an incentive.[4]

With the recognition that the appeal of monetary incentives was limited, attention turned to the workers' physical environment. The Scientific Management School was at the forefront of this trend. This school viewed the physical environment and monetary incentives as closely linked, in that morale would be improved by pleasant surroundings, thus leading to greater production, which in turn would lead to greater pay. Ironically, the concern with surroundings was responsible for the discovery of the importance of the human element in organizational behavior. The well-known Hawthorne studies at Western Electric were directed at finding the optimal physical conditions under which assembly line workers could produce. Experiments in changing illumination levels and other aspects of the work environment led to the discovery that psychological factors were more important than were physical conditions in determining levels of productivity.[5]

The human relations approach to management, focusing on people's social nature, grew out of the Hawthorne studies. Creating a work situation in which employees feel that management cares about them is supposed to lead to greater productivity. Fostering interpersonal relationships and group dynamics became the fad of the immediate post–World II era. Students of organization emphasized the informal groups and norms in organizations and frequently ignored the formal structure.[6] Most studies in the human relations areas concentrated on the way the requirements of the formal structure created unnatural specialization and led to the development of informal groups to overcome the tediousness of work. Little attention was given to the need for reevaluating the work process itself; managers were supposed to become the friends of the workers. Such approaches led to charges that employees were being manipulated by human relations programs, and workers saw through managers whose interest was still that of increasing productivity—only now it was through psychological rather than monetary means. Although the human relations approach certainly helped humanize the work situation, it still focused on the individual as a part of the organization's machinery. One student of management, Chester I. Barnard, saw very early that the requirements of the individual and the organization had to be matched in some way.[7] Nonetheless, his focus was on motivating workers by means of effective management techniques and leadership qualities. For some time, leadership traits and styles were seen as the principal reasons for gaining the employees' cooperation. Particularly important to students of organizations was the style of leadership used. Generally, it was concluded that the democratic style is most effective over the long run; authoritarian leadership may be effective over the short term; and laissez-faire leadership seems to be ineffective.[8] Barnard combined his research on leadership with the reactions of employees to their leader and was an early advocate of considering the personality of workers and managers as well as the psychological factors in the workers' reactions to commands and directives. It was therefore a short step to studies on the relationship between human personality and organizations.

The organizational humanists, typified by Chris Argyris, tried to go beyond the manipulative approaches of human relations and to identify the needs of individuals that affect their roles as members of organizations.[9] In essence, Argyris claimed that organizations require submissive and dependent workers who will do as they are told; the incongruity between personality and organization needs becomes greater the lower one is in the hierarchy. Argyris called for organizations to adapt in order to promote greater responsibility for their members. In recent years, as we shall discuss shortly, many others have built on his approach, and numerous programs have been introduced to capitalize on the abilities of workers long neglected by traditional approaches.

Argyris argued that not all people react in the same way but that many needs of the mature human personality are inconsistent with the demands of organizations modeled on traditional principles. Robert Presthus, among others, pointed out that personalities differed in their adjustments to the needs of complex organizations.[10] Once the ground was broken, however, a whole new approach to maximizing individuals' potential was unleashed. People were no longer viewed as disliking their work per se; rather, the way their work was organized was the culprit. People could be motivated to produce if they were permitted to develop themselves in their work situation. Behavioral scientists have built on these ideas to devise new approaches to human self-actualization in the work place. The next section of this chapter will summarize some of their approaches.

The work of Presthus and others led to the recognition that different types of personalities are found in different levels of organizations. Those at the highest levels of management are usually less concerned with material rewards and the need to feel wanted by the organization than they are with recognition, prestige, credentials, or the accumulation of the symbols of success. The relationship of these persons' success inside the organization to success or recognition in society as a whole may be much more of a driving force than for those in the middle and lower levels of the bureaucracy.[11]

The behavioral approach stresses that human beings enjoy and need work as much as they do recreation; therefore, ways should be found to permit employees to use their capacities to their fullest in the work situation.[12] The key to effective organization became what Douglas McGregor called the Theory Y form of organization, stressing people's independence, creative ability, intelligence, and willingness to perform what they view as useful tasks. The realization that people do not hate work, are capable of making intelligent judgments, and are motivated to achieve objectives that they have a part in determining has led to the advocacy by many of democratic, or participative, administration.

Behavioral scientists base their analysis on the belief that individuals have a hierarchy of needs—physiological, safety, social, ego, and self-actualization, in that order.[13] As each need is satisfied, it ceases to be a motivator, and the next higher one takes its place. Frederick Herzberg suggested that most organizations do not actually build on these needs as motivators; rather, they tend to focus on "hygiene" factors—physical surroundings, status, and the like—which all members of an organization expect anyway.[14] Basing his analysis on the hierarchy of human needs, Herzberg recommended that organizations use positive growth factors as motivators because the workers' motivation comes only from such things as their own achievement, recognition, and increased responsibility.[15]

Motivating employees through behavioral science approaches involves a variety of techniques, some specifically motivational in intent and others more generally concerned with humanizing the organization. One of the most general and most widely accepted behavioral conclusions is that employees will be more committed and more productive if they have the opportunity to participate in the organization's decisions, particularly those pertaining to the work situation. Democratization of the work place is often advocated but not easily implemented, especially in the public sector. The meaning of employee participation in the decision-making process is often vague. The human relations approach frequently suggested participative processes, but most efforts seemed to be cosmetic attempts to convince employees that they were important. Managers often resist real employee participation because they are not trained in behavioral techniques and are unsure about their proper roles in the new approaches.

Management-by-objectives (MBO) is one popular participative management approach and involves agreement on objectives by the organization's members. Decision making may be on the unit level or, in smaller organizations, may encompass the organization as a whole. Studies by Robert Ford and others indicate that employees set higher goals for themselves than management would set, but more importantly, the employees have a stake in meeting the goals and are motivated to prove themselves.[16] MBO has been used chiefly in the private sector, but it has had some application in public agencies. However, there are constraints on its use in the public sector, such as the unpredictability of annual budget allocations, the high rate of turnover of top political executives, and constantly changing priorities. Moreover, political realities may bring about new program goals and emphases.

Job enrichment is another motivational technique suggested by many behavioral scientists. Job boredom seems to be a major problem in all sectors and levels of society but particularly for lower-level employees.[17] By making the job interesting, management can obtain greater commitment and motivation from the employees. Employees who have control over and responsibility for their work, who see the results of their efforts, and who have diversified duties are likely to identify with the job and take pride in doing it well. They are also likely to be more productive than those who perform a highly specialized task with no idea about the end product.[18] Although most behavioral theorists recognize the advantages of job enrichment, they are usually imprecise in outlining methods of implementing it. Managers find the principle difficult to apply, but as with participatory management, the reasons for resistance are usually lack of understanding of the technique and unfounded fears of loss of status or role.

Associated with the motivation theory are a number of experimental movements known as T-group, sensitivity training, or encounter sessions. These all are part of a larger movement known variously as organization development, organization change, or organization renewal. The focus in much of the literature is on adapting the organization to the changing environment and, particularly relevant to our considerations, to the changing needs of the people within the organization.[19] The idea of organization development is to break down barriers to effective communication. The hope is that through self-awareness and the awareness of others and organization needs, all the individuals in the organization will become more trusting of one another, more committed to the organization's goals, and more self-directed and responsible in attempting to solve organizational problems.[20] In general, the approach is based on the assumption that people will change their attitudes and behavior for the better if there is an open problem-solving atmosphere.

Such a program endeavors to help employees realize their full capacities. Many agencies use organization development techniques, but there are often limitations to its use in the public sector. Of primary concern are the political forces under which public agencies operate. Explaining the value of encounter sessions to a legislator who gets a complaint from a disgruntled employee is not easy. And justifying such use of tax money to a legislative body or to the general public is not relished by most public administrators; therefore they are not always eager to adopt such programs. Because of the bad image of many organization development programs, there is a greater emphasis now on training seminars and in-house training programs in which people are asked to evaluate their organizations in open sessions in which personality factors are minimized. Still, there are problems, particularly when the programs consist of short training sessions without follow-up programs to continue the process.

The traditional methods of motivating employees use rewards and punishments. Behavior modification employs some of these traditional approaches through positive reinforcers, negative reinforcers, and/or punishers.[21] Money, bonuses, promotions, and the like are promised for improved productivity, and less pay or less desirable duties are used to penalize poor performance. Feedback to the employee on performance is essential in such a system; thus, it is necessary that specific performance measures be devised.

Another recent addition to behavioral techniques in organizations is the quality circle concept. Although it uses many of the well-established behavioral principles, the approach has been embraced as a new way of motivating employees. Quality Circles have been used successfully in Japan after the Japanese imported the idea from the United States shortly after World War II. Seeing the success in Japan, many United States industries reimported the concept during the 1970s, and the public sector has experimented with Quality Circles as well. The concept involves developing work groups in organizational units whose main purpose is to improve their quality of performance. Through participative techniques and a consensus on how best to do the unit's work, the work groups provide a sense of commitment to the organization and its goals. As with all other behavioral techniques, Quality Circles work only as well as the quality of the management and personnel of the organization permit them to work.

Behavioral approaches to motivating employees have produced a number of techniques. Unfortunately, many achieve the status of fads, and the experiments have often failed and even exacerbated problems. The most common complaints suggest that managers are not trained in behavioral techniques and think that they can implement various organization development approaches after attending a short training session. More often than not, the results are disastrous for both the employees and the supervisors. Even though the supervisors may believe in the program, their attitudes toward their employees may be the same as they always were. Harry Levinson believes that another problem is that the sharing of power, implicit in organization development approaches, contradicts the manager's role expectations and personality.[22]

Another common criticism of the behavioral approaches is that they are viewed as panaceas for all organization problems and that particular techniques are adopted because of their faddishness rather than because they fit the organization's problems. To avoid such inappropriate uses of behavioral techniques, the needs of the organization, personnel, and management should be assessed, and then the appropriate technique can be determined.

There are no easy answers to the questions of how to motivate employees. Basically, however, managers need to recognize that they are dealing with people who have diverse needs, who consider their work to be a natural part of their lives, who react differently to the same situation, and who can be motivated primarily from within. An environment in which people can develop themselves to their fullest usually provides the best opportunity for motivation. In addition, managers must consider the organization and the level of the individual in it. What motivates the top-level manager is not likely to motivate the worker whose job calls for little thought and much repetition. Similarly, the value systems discussed earlier influence the receptivity of individual workers to various motivational techniques.

Productivity Improvement

A major aspect of performance improvement is productivity improvement. Concern with productivity and productivity improvements has almost become a fad, although the specific elements of given programs have long been around in different forms. Productivity refers to the efficiency with which resources are consumed in the effective delivery of service.[23] Thus productivity encompasses both the quality and the quantity of output produced for any given input of resources, but it also refers to the output's effectiveness. Whether the service or the product is needed or of value has become increasingly important, especially in the public sector. Public managers are under ever-mounting pressures to increase the productivity of their organizations, as taxpayers demand more services and lower taxes.

As with performance generally, productivity depends on the technology used, the work force, and the management. Each of these elements of the public service can contribute to or obstruct productivity. Perhaps the simplest method of improving productivity is to improve the technology available to the work forces. For example, containerized trash collection or computerized record keeping can increase the amount or quality of work while maintaining or even decreasing the resources required. There are, however, limits to the amount of improvement that technology can produce.

Improved management can also contribute to productivity improvement. The behavioral techniques just discussed are expected to lead to increased organizational performance; thus training managers in better managerial techniques is usually inspired by expectations of better organizational productivity. Typical areas of improvement are in communications, lines of authority, and involvement of employees in decision making.

Employees, and especially employee unions, are often suspicious of productivity improvement programs that are unilaterally imposed by management. In fact, such programs are often viewed as a throwback to the piece-rate days preceding unionization in the private sector or as an effort to either reduce service or increase the employees' work load. In the face of employee opposition, such programs are almost certainly doomed to failure, as the employees are the ones who will have to increase their effort if they are to be successful.

Employee participation appears to be a major factor in the success of improvement plans, and employees seem to respond best to those programs that protect their job security and job satisfaction. As we noted in our discussion of motivation, employees are most likely to be committed to programs in which they have a say. This commitment is usually translated into greater effort and thus greater productivity. Again, employees often resent unilateral attempts by management to increase their productivity and either sabotage or ignore such efforts.

One way in which employees participate in productivity improvement is through collective bargaining, in what is known as productivity bargaining. Productivity bargaining, as defined by Chester A. Newland, is "the negotiation and implementation of formal collective bargaining agreements which stipulate changes in work rules and practices with the objective of achieving increased productivity and reciprocal worker gains."[25] As the process is implemented, employees change to more efficient work practices in return for a share of the organization's savings produced by the greater productivity. In theory, everyone benefits: management eliminates inefficiency; employees receive pay increases or other benefits; and the public enjoys the improved quality and quantity of public services. Experience uncovers many problem areas.

Discussions of difficulties in productivity bargaining are plentiful in the literature on the public sector. Some of the problems are intrinsic to productivity standards, whereas others apply directly to the bargaining process. The major criticism and issues raised revolve around problems in measuring productivity, management's giving up its prerogatives to manage, and the idea that the public is being asked to pay more to persuade employees to do what they were hired to do in the first place.

Productivity measurements in the public sector pose a problem because many public services cannot easily be quantified. The service orientation of government implies that results or outcomes are most important, whereas most productivity measures emphasize activities. Despite the problems, many measures are readily available, and indicators of productivity in less tangible service areas can be developed with some effort. Perhaps more important is that there is not always agreement about what the organization's goals are or should be, and thus measuring performance becomes more confused. Nonetheless, program evaluation techniques are more and more often applied to measuring the performance of public agencies.

Care is necessary to ensure that the quantitative factors that ignore quality do not become the only considerations in measuring productivity. Productivity bargaining can affect the priorities of employees in performing their duties and possibly hinder their general service to the public. The following example illustrates some of the possible adverse effects of overemphasizing specific measurable activities.

Productivity bargaining normally produces agreements specifying that employees will receive certain benefits (pay increases, reduction in working hours, more vacation, and so on) for a given demonstrated increase in productivity. Because productivity measures are not yet very sophisticated, there is a tendency to use certain fairly easily measured activities as indicators of productivity. Paul D. Staudohar examined a productivity bargaining agreement that the city of Orange, California, worked out with its unionized police force.[26] The city and union agreed to use four easily quantifiable aspects of police activity to indicate productivity. The police were to earn pay increases based on reductions in the incidence of rape, burglary, robbery, and auto theft. Subsequently, the incidence of burglary and rape decreased, though robbery and auto theft actually increased. The decrease in burglary and rape was large enough, however, to offset the others, and the police received the maximum pay increase provided for by the agreement.

Although the results that Staudohar reported offered encouragement in one way—the reduction of certain crimes—they also had potentially adverse aspects. One difficulty is that police officers not only fight crime but also offer numerous services to the public. Even within the crime-fighting function, there are many crimes other than the four singled out in the Orange experiment. Nonetheless, the agreement rewarded officers only for improved performance in those areas.

It seems only natural that overall performance would be sacrificed to produce a good record on the items cited in the bargaining agreement. As Peter Blau demonstrated in examining performance evaluation, using particular parts of employee performance as criteria for increased pay or promotion leads employees to focus on establishing a good record on those criteria that count in their favor.[27] Because productivity measures are simply alternative means for measuring performance, the same effects can be expected with productivity bargaining. In order to minimize distortions in performance, agreements might include provisions that the overall level of productivity remain the same as specific indicators show improvement. But if the overall quality of service declines, it hardly seems appropriate to reward employees for improving only certain aspects of their performance. Such provisions will depend, of course, on management's ability to measure all aspects of productivity.

Another approach, "total performance measurement," is being used to cope with some of the pitfalls of productivity improvement programs.[28] This approach uses productivity data, along with other information, to evaluate overall performance and improve productivity. Employees, clientele, and citizens are surveyed to determine whether the organization is perceived as being productive and its service is effective and useful. Data on productivity are also evaluated. Feedback to employees and managers is a central focus of total performance measurement. Such feedback permits everyone to understand what needs change and encourages participation in making the changes. This approach differs from others primarily in the systematic way in which data are collected and used. Otherwise, it uses techniques already contained in other approaches.

Performance Evaluation

Performance evaluation is an essential yet difficult part of the personnel process. During periods of cutbacks in funding and pressures for increased productivity, performance evaluation is particularly important. As Albert Hyde noted, performance evaluation serves different purposes, depending on whether it is viewed from the perspective of management or the employee.[29] Management or the organization is concerned with using performance evaluation to improve performance and to make decisions about compensation, training needs, and improving management. Viewed from the individual perspective, however, performance evaluation assumes importance in considerations of equity, employee growth and development, and participation and support of human resources in the organization. These conflicting perspectives can lead to a misunderstanding of the performance evaluation system and anxiety for the employee and supervisor alike.[30]

The basic responsibility for performance evaluation rests with the supervisor or manager, though recent trends have also included the employee in the evaluation process. Employees are often asked to rate themselves on their performance and then to discuss their evaluation with their supervisor and compare it with the supervisor's appraisal. In many cases, the employee actually sets up goals and objectives with the supervisor and then is evaluated against them.

Regardless of how the evaluations are made, they tend to cause anxiety. Supervisors often have difficulty explaining exactly what is expected of their employees in the first place, and when evaluation time comes, they have difficulty measuring performance against what they see as the organization's goals. It is usually assumed that the supervisors' anxiety arises because of their not wanting to deliver bad news to the employee, but John Nalbandian found that supervisors are actually most uncomfortable with their subordinates' reaction to their evaluation.[31] It is to be expected that employees will be defensive about their evaluation and that supervisors will become uncomfortable in dealing with those reactions.

The inclination in recent years has been to formalize the evaluation process. Whereas in years past, informal approaches with little record keeping sufficed, modern times require more documentation. Thus, annual evaluations are common, with a formal report being kept in the employee's personnel file. With increasing pressures from employee organizations, the law, and the courts requiring that performance evaluation and other personnel functions be based on valid job-related criteria, supervisors must regularize the process and protect the organization and the employee both.[32]

Performance ratings can take various forms, such as the measurement of output or examinations. Numerical ratings on various characteristics such as punctuality, attitude, and ability to work with others are common, as are narrative or essay evaluations. Each of these approaches has numerous variations and negative and positive features. For example, output measurement may be effective in evaluating performance when an identifiable product is made, but it is inappropriate when service or policy is the output. Examinations are useful in measuring potential or capacity, but they may be ineffectual in judging actual performance.

Rating employees on various qualities and narrative evaluations can be effective if they are carefully constructed and properly used.[33] The checkoff, or objective evaluation, assigns employees a score on such qualities as promptness, courtesy, writing ability, and initiative. The narrative approach permits supervisors to describe the employees' strong and weak points. In some narrative evaluations, specific items must be discussed. These evaluation techniques are not very popular because they are difficult to compare and there is little control over what qualities are evaluated. Rating people on specific qualities is easier and provides for greater comparability. Unfortunately, the qualities rated often have little relevance to performance; rather, they often relate to personal traits. Although personality factors may be important to some jobs, such is not the case for all or even most positions. A recent study by Tyer found that state governments are shifting toward performance-based evaluation systems.[34] Of course, the Civil Service Reform Act of 1978 requires each department to develop a performance-based appraisal system.

Several methods of evaluation incorporate elements of both the rating and the narrative approaches. The critical incident type of evaluation has the supervisor record specific behaviors of the employee that are indicative of good or bad performance. This method highlights performance-related activities and thus conforms to one of the major criteria necessary for effective evaluation. However, it tends to focus on behavior extremes and, as such, may ignore the overall, less visible aspects of performance that might tell more about the employee's role in the organization. Thus the employee who does well consistently but seldom does anything spectacular may be at a disadvantage.

The narrative approach has many variations as well. It may require the supervisor to write an overall evaluation of the employee's performance, or it may require an explanation of the employee's most significant contribution to the organization and most serious weakness. Or it may call for a description of specific factors such as quality of work, ability to get along with others, innovation, and potential for growth. As noted, these approaches usually are not good for comparing employees, but they do offer flexibility and an opportunity for supervisors to stress individual contributions and provide a broader perspective on performance. One drawback is that supervisors vary in their ability to identify strengths and weaknesses and then write about them. The employee then benefits or suffers according to the supervisor's skills.

Forced-choice evaluation is another approach. In this method the supervisor may be required to choose a certain percentage of employees who deserve recognition for meritorious performance. Such an approach is often used in merit pay decisions in which perhaps one-half, one-third, or one-fourth of a supervisor's subordinates may be singled out for merit pay increases. It usually forces the supervisor to develop specific criteria by which the decisions are made. It is not, however, an easy process to administer and can create morale problems.

In recent years, many organizations have used group and peer appraisal. Peer appraisal may use any of the forms suggested above but frequently requires a numerical rating on specific characteristics. It often also entails a simple listing of those individuals who should be considered good and poor workers. This method can offer illuminating perspectives on employee performance, though it may produce inflated evaluations.

In the self-appraisal system, employees examine their own performance relative to specified criteria. In most instances, they then discuss their evaluation with their supervisor. Employees tend to judge themselves relatively harshly and cannot always see themselves in relation to the total organization; thus their evaluations can be incorrect. Nonetheless, used in combination with other techniques, they can provide a useful examination of employee activities.

Performance evaluations can distort the importance of particular activities to the organization. For instance, if output is the major criterion on which employees are evaluated, it is not surprising that employees will neglect other concerns such as coordination of effort or quality of output. The likelihood is that employees will focus on the activities that gain them favorable evaluations.[35]

Perhaps the greatest problem with performance ratings is that they often are made hurriedly and periodically. When the deadline for evaluations approaches, the supervisor does them quickly, often remembering only the exceptional or most recent occurrences. The result is a distorted view of the employee. Ongoing evaluations in which the supervisor discusses the strong and weak aspects of performance as they occur is probably the most effective approach. The employee can then make adjustments as needed rather than finding at the end of a year that he or she has not lived up to expectations. Adequate record keeping is also necessary. If an employee does not correct unsatisfactory performance over a reasonable period of time, disciplinary action is in order. Similarly, when the employee feels that he or she has been unfairly judged, a review process should be available. Most importantly, evaluations should have as their goal the best performance possible, and punishment should be a last resort.

In recent years, performance evaluations have served to protect employees from capricious action by their superiors. A record of periodic evaluations makes it difficult for the supervisor to suddenly dismiss an employee who is out of favor. In the days when employees were not regularly evaluated, they could be told after a number of years of service that they did not meet the (often unspecified) standards of the agency. Similarly, a record of inadequate performance can be used in disciplining and terminating employees.

Discipline

Disciplining employees is a task that most supervisors would rather avoid. If the organization has effective personnel policies in general, discipline should be needed only on rare occasions. Because of the spotlight in which the public service must operate, however, public employers must often judge their employees by higher standards of conduct than are found in the private sector.

An effective discipline policy is one that is clearly stated, clearly understood by employees, and uniformly applied. If discipline is not timely, any later actions are likely to be ineffectual. In addition, unjust disciplinary actions are likely to be resented and to be destructive to morale. But once such actions are imposed, the employee should have access to an appeal process to review the disciplinary action in order to protect against capricious action by supervisors.

The most commonly used forms of discipline are reprimands, suspension (with or without pay), demotion or other reassignment, and removal. Others used to a lesser degree include loss of salary increases, seniority rights, overtime work, or demerits on the employee's personnel record. These latter forms of discipline were once used extensively but are now considered demeaning and not particularly productive.

Reprimands, both oral and written, should be enough to correct most problems, particularly if there is good communication and mutual respect between the employee and the supervisor. The purpose of the reprimand should be to correct the employee's actions and not to embarrass or humiliate the person. The supervisor's training and personality are important to making this type of disciplinary action effective. A fumbling and inconsiderate use of reprimands can cause irreparable harm to employee–supervisor relations.

Suspension, demotion, and reassignment are more severe types of discipline. They should be used with care and only if reprimands are ineffective. Suspension often leaves the employee with a loss of pay and may only kindle hostility. Demotion and reassignment are appropriate when the employee has demonstrated a lack of ability in a particular position. The change of job is ordinarily made on the basis of more effectively utilizing the employee's capabilities. Using it as a disciplinary action is humiliating to employees and only makes them more resistant to the organization and its needs. Reassignment may result in the pawning off of incompetent employees on other units of the organization and thus weakening the organization as a whole.

Removal is the most extreme penalty and should be used only as a last resort. Dismissal policies should be clearly stated and understood, as with all disciplinary policies. Employees' appeal rights are routine parts of such policies. Too much procedural detail, however, may lead to inflexibility for the manager. A balance between the rights of the employees and the expectations of the public of quality service is often difficult to achieve. Managers often feel frustrated at the difficulties of disciplining employees. As Arthur Finkle demonstrated, there are many obstacles to taking disciplinary action against incompetent or nonperforming employees.[36]

At the same time, there are many problems with managers harassing employees just for differing with them or the agency policy. The Civil Service Reform Act of 1978 attempted to protect employees from such badgering and contains a provision to protect "whistle blowers," or people who inform on the wrongful behavior of their supervisors and agencies. The act prohibits reprisals against whistle blowers and provides for bringing disciplinary charges against those who institute such reprisals. But neither the Carter nor the Reagan administrations showed much support for the provision, and so employees are still vulnerable.

Employee Training and Development

In the past, governments assumed that they could acquire personnel in the labor market with the requisite skills and abilities; therefore, the training and development of public employees was not considered a high priority. In recent years, however, technological change, recognition of the need for employees to improve themselves, and affirmative action and equal employment opportunity programs brought pressure for training programs by government employers. In addition, the public service often requires skills not readily available in the labor market. The national government passed the Government Employees Training Act of 1958 which calls on federal agencies to draw up programs, and the Intergovernmental Personnel Act of 1970 funded many programs for state and local government training and development. Despite the elimination of that program by the Reagan administration, state and local governments have assumed the responsibility for training themselves.

When instituting a training program, the personnel agency and operating department usually work together, although in some units of government, the training function is separate from the personnel agency. The personnel agency or training unit can provide the expertise and advice for the programs, but the operating department is usually in the best position to determine the actual training needs. A centralized training agency usually has the needs-assessment capabilities as well as the training competence. Many training programs use both central agency and operating department people and facilities.

The most elementary training program is a new-employee orientation program which can have a significant impact on behavior and productivity.[37] Traditionally, agencies spent a short time introducing new employees and explaining the rules, regulations, and benefits of the job. Now the orientation process is often stretched out over a longer period—depending on the job, of course—and employees are encouraged to discuss their problems in adjusting to and learning their duties. The result is that employees become more productive more quickly.

On-the-job training is another approach. An individual without the needed skills is hired and learns the job from another employee. Often the person serves an apprenticeship. Such training may also be used to help employees move up in their organizations by learning new skills.

It has become common to encourage individual employee development through a variety of programs inside and outside the organization. The main beneficiaries of such programs are frequently supervisors and managers, but many other employees have benefited as well. These programs take the form of workshops, institutes, professional conferences, university and college programs, and sabbaticals. The national government has sponsored such programs for a long time and permits state and local government employees to participate in many of the federal programs. State and local governments have also drawn up many of their own programs along the same lines. Not surprisingly, the national government has been a leader in many types of training programs. The Office of Personnel Management sponsors a variety of programs and has training centers in each of its regions. Although the regional centers are primarily for middle- and upper-level federal officials, state and local personnel may also be accepted on a space-available basis. Executive Seminar Centers in various parts of the country provide opportunities for intensive programs for management personnel. The Federal Executive Institute at Charlottesville, Virginia, offers small, intensive courses for high-level administrators and shows the OPM's commitment to excellence in the public service. In addition to these programs, individual departments and agencies conduct their own training and development activities.

Although state and local governments were slow to follow the national government's lead, most have now established some sort of ongoing training program. The Intergovernmental Personnel Act of 1970 provided the seed money for many training and development activities and demonstrated the value of such activities. Of course, training and development programs often fall victim to budget cuts, and in times when finances are limited, these programs suffer. Nonetheless, training and development have been recognized as essential efforts in the public service at all levels of government.

Mobility programs train employees in a broad area of activities. In the national government, for example, the Senior Executive Service (SES) is one example of mobility. Though its emphasis is not on training, it does permit those selected to be exposed to a large part of the federal bureaucracy and thus broaden their skills and knowledge. Mobility programs were a significant part of the Intergovernmental Personnel Act programs. Employees of state and local governments would often take temporary assignments in the federal bureaucracy, and federal government employees would do the same in state or local governments. Universities also participated in the program. Now, individual federal government agencies maintain similar efforts, and the private sector sometimes becomes involved as well. For example, in Arizona, members of the private sector occasionally spend a specified period of time working with a public sector agency. These programs help employees learn about the other organizations they deal with and also offer opportunities to employees to develop new skills and expertise that can be important to their agencies. The participating organizations also benefit from the new perspectives of the people they host.

A type of training aimed at new and prospective employees is the internship. Many institutions of higher education require public service internships as part of their undergraduate and graduate programs in public administration. Other disciplines have their own internships as well. Students gain experience in the practical application of what they learn in the classroom. The internship requires the willingness of government agencies to budget money for them and to supervise the interns they host. Of course, the agencies benefit along with the student if the internship is carefully planned and executed. The Presidential Management Internship at the national level is an example of a major internship program in which top students from across the country are recruited to spend two years with a federal agency, with the expectation that the interns will become permanent employees. Several states, including Texas and Montana, have copied this program. Dallas, Kansas City, Long Beach, Phoenix, and the metropolitan Dade County government have similar programs at the local level.

Training is costly, and the costs lead to controversy over whether training should even be undertaken. The long-term costs to the organization of not undertaking training may be greater, however, and most governments have recognized the value of such programs. A lack of training leads to employees with outmoded skills who are likely to become frustrated at the lack of growth opportunity. The end result is the necessity of recruiting new employees, which is a costly process.

Performance Under Fiscal Constraints

Fiscal constraints are facts of life for governments at all levels. Tax revolts and other spending limitations became popular in the late 1970s and spread nationwide, necessitating cutback management in government. In order to deal with these pressures, governments have looked to the personnel function as a major concern, as personnel costs are the single most expensive part of governments' operating costs. Cutback management creates many uncertainties and faces resistance from employees, their unions, interest groups, and the agency managers themselves. Attempting to accommodate the varying interests of these actors in the process as well as to satisfy the demands of the public and politically elected officials places the personnel function in a difficult position. Reductions-in-force and contracting out for public services are two major strategies used in cutback management.

When faced with cutbacks in funds, most governmental units attempt some form of reduction in their work force. Reduction-in-force (RIF) may be accomplished through layoffs or attrition. Layoffs mean that positions are identified as dispensable according to criteria on which the unit agrees, and attrition means that positions are eliminated or not filled as incumbents leave them for whatever reason. Each method of achieving a reduction in force leads to both positive and negative results for the organization.[38]

Layoffs have the advantage of permitting the agency to reduce the size of its personnel force quickly and in those positions it identifies as dispensable. Thus, if conducted with a clear evaluation of an agency's needs and resources, layoffs can lead to a streamlined agency that is better able to use the skills and expertise of the employees it retains. Unfortunately, the task is not so easy as it may sound. Establishing the criteria for layoffs is usually a very controversial process. Usually, employee unions want the decision rule for layoffs to be seniority, whereas management usually wants some other criterion, such as performance or contribution to the organization's needs. If the criteria depend on the evaluation of performance or the like, uncertainty is likely to develop among the employees, and morale problems may arise. Along with the loss of morale and the employees' insecurity, productivity is likely to decline as well.

Cutbacks through layoffs do provide the opportunity for management to evaluate the agency and its employees and thus to find ways to use the agency's resources more efficiently in achieving the organization's goals. The evidence suggests, however, that layoffs usually do not occur as a result of such rational analysis and often lead to greater problems for the organization because of the employees' insecurity regarding the process.[39] The public service and the citizens also do not benefit much from poorly planned and executed RIF systems.

Attrition usually is looked upon more favorably by employees and their unions than are layoffs, because no one loses her or his job involuntarily. Instead, as people leave, their positions are not filled. Management usually does not oppose attrition either, in that it eases management's job in getting the cooperation of employees in the RIF. Some managers, however, recognize that attrition can cause significant problems for the organization if it is not well planned and implemented. A basic problem is that management cannot control which positions are going to become vacant. Employees leave for a variety of reasons, and often the most valuable employees are best able to acquire new jobs. As a result, the employees with the most sought-after skill or best performance record may leave, and management is left with those who are not very marketable. Obviously, the organization's productivity will suffer if such is the case.

But attrition can be an effective reduction-in-force method if the organization prepares for it. Employees can be cross-trained so that if some leave, others will be able to pick up their responsibilities. Especially effective is the training of those employees whose skills or positions are least valuable to the organization's work. They can be trained in more needed areas of activity and thus become valuable to the organization. Similarly, if needed skills are lost through attrition, internal training can be used to fill the need. The training may also have another advantage in that it gives the trainees a better perspective on the organization: they may see it as an organization that cares about them and so become more committed to its goals.

Clearly, layoffs and attrition can accomplish the objectives of reducing the number of personnel in a governmental unit. The choice of system depends on the particular situation and the speed with which reduction is necessary. Given the more humanistic nature of most personnel systems these days, attrition seems to be the most common method of achieving a reduction in force. The effects on the employees' performance usually loom large in the decision as to which method to use.

Another method of achieving cutbacks in government spending is using contracting out for government service. Contracting is often touted as a cost saver in that it reduces the permanent personnel of the governmental unit and permits the unit to contract for exactly the amount of service required. Thus, it is unnecessary to maintain large work forces in anticipation of a heavy work load that does not materialize or for seasonal jobs such as snow removal. Instead, the governmental unit can contract for the job, and the private employer bears the cost of the overhead for maintaining its payroll. Too, a private employer performing the service for many governments or other private organizations may realize economies of scale which can be reflected in the cost of the contract. It is also usually assumed that governmental jurisdictions save because they do not get tied into long-term benefit programs, such as retirement programs for the employees. The private firm handles all of that. Of course, contracting may be done with other governmental jurisdictions as well as with private firms.[40]

Although contracting out for services seems to have many cost advantages, not everyone agrees with the proponents' rosy picture. The American Federation of State, County, and Municipal Employees (AFSCME), for instance, believes that in the long run, contracting for services is likely to cost taxpayers more.[41] AFSCME points to problems in controlling the cost and quality of the service provided and the potential for collusion between public officials and contractors. These potential abuses can cost the taxpayer, and the costs of monitoring and making the contractors accountable must be borne by the taxpayer. Obviously, AFSCME has a special interest in protecting the jobs of public employees, but it does raise some issues that governments need to consider when they do contract out for services.

Summary

Public employee performance is a key concern of governments because taxpayers demand high levels of service while attempting to hold the line on taxes. To ensure the highest level of service possible, public employers depend on the supervisor to create an environment in which employees wish to work. In addition, organizations use various theories of motivation to persuade employees to produce at their optimum. In recent years, behavioral approaches to organizing the work unit and job have acquired much support as ways of improving productivity. Governments also use productivity improvement programs utilizing new technology, better management, and employee participation. Evaluation systems test the performance of employees and the effects of techniques for improving productivity. Performance evaluation also helps determine the need for training and development programs to improve the skills and opportunities of employees in the organization.

Public employers are limited in their ability to use performance enhancement measures by the realities of the political environment. The political environment of the 1980s is dominated by pressures for fiscal constraint. Thus, public employers must find ways of doing the job better while having fewer resources with which to work. The result is that governments must reduce the number of government personnel while still trying to meet the public's demands for service. The employer therefore is caught between the demands of the employees and those of the citizens. Cutback management is accomplished through reduction-in-force methods (layoffs and attrition) and contracting for services. Of course, some services are also eliminated and are accompanied by reductions in force.

NOTES

1. For a study of how important supervision is, see George C. Homans, "Effort, Supervision, and Productivity," in Robert T. Golembiewski and Michael Cohen, eds., *People in Public Service* (Itasca, Ill.: Peacock, 1976), pp. 248–259; originally published in Robert Dulim, ed., *Leadership and Productivity* (San Francisco: Chandler, 1965), pp. 51–67.

2. For a detailed examination of these and other tasks, see International City Manager's Association, *Effective Supervisory Practices*, 2nd ed. (Washington, D.C.: International City Manager's Association, 1978).

3. For an entertaining look at problems of promotion in organizations and how to deal with them, see Lawrence J. Peter, *The Peter Prescription* (New York: Morrow, 1972).

4. William Foote Whyte et al., *Money and Motivation* (New York: Harper & Row, 1955) is one of the major works on this issue.

5. The Hawthorne studies have been widely reported in public administration literature, and so they will not be described here. But for an analysis, readers may wish to check J. A. C. Brown, *The Social Psychology of Industry* (Baltimore: Penguin, 1962); or George C. Homans, "The Western Electric Research," in Schuyler Dean Hoslett, ed., *Human Factors in Management*, rev. ed. (New York: Harper & Row, 1951). A new perspective on the studies is also offered by H. M. Parsons, "What Happened at Hawthorne?" *Science*, March 8, 1974, pp. 922–932.

6. One of the leaders in informal organization research is Peter Blau, who has two major works in the area: *The Dynamics of Bureaucracy: A Study of Interpersonal Relationships in Two Government Agencies*, 2nd ed. (Chicago: University of Chicago Press, 1963); and with Marshall W. Mayer, *Bureaucracy in Modern Society*, 2nd ed. (New York: Random House, 1971).

7. Chester I. Barnard, *The Functions of the Executive* (Cambridge, Mass.: Harvard University Press, 1968, originally published in 1938).

8. The evidence is mixed. See Ronald Lippitt and Ralph White, "An Experimental Study of Leadership and Group Life," in T. M. Newcomb and E. L. Hartley, eds., *Readings in Social Psychology* (New York: Holt, Rinehart & Winston, 1947); Robert T. Golembiewski, "Three Styles of Leadership and Their Uses," *Personnel*, 38 (July-August 1961), 35–42; Rensis Likert, *The Human Organization: Its Management and Value* (New York: McGraw-Hill, 1967); and Gerald T. Gabris and William A. Giles, "Perceptions of Management Style and Employee Performance: Resurrecting a Diminishing Debate," *Public Personnel Management*, 12 (Summer 1983), 167–180.

9. Argyris has written several books and articles on the issue, but the most exhaustive is *Integrating the Individual and Organization* (New York: John Wiley, 1964).

10. Robert Presthus, *The Organizational Society*, rev. ed. (New York: St. Martin's Press, 1978).

11. Anthony Downs, *Inside Bureaucracy* (Boston: Little, Brown, 1967), pp. 81–91 and chap. 9, has some interesting observations on this issue. Also see Peter Rand, "Collecting Merit Badges: The White House Fellows," *Washington Monthly*, 6 (June 1974), 47–56, for an excellent evaluation of the motives and pressures for achievement.

12. Perhaps the seminal work on this issue is by Douglas McGregor, *The Human Side of Enterprise* (New York: McGraw-Hill, 1968).

13. Based on Abraham Maslow, *Motivation and Personality* (New York: Harper & Row, 1954).

14. Frederick Herzberg, *Work and the Nature of Man* (Cleveland: World Publishing, 1966), especially chap. 3.

15. Ibid., chaps. 6–9 explain his theory. Also see Frederick Herzberg, "One More Time: How Do You Motivate Employees?" *Harvard Business Review*, 46 (January-February 1968), 53–57.

16. Robert N. Ford, *Motivation Through the Work Itself* (New York: American Management Association, 1969), cites many examples at AT&T, for instance.

17. See *Work in America*, Report of a Special Task Force to the Secretary of Health, Education and Welfare (Cambridge, Mass.: MIT Press, 1973) for a discussion of worker dissatisfaction and boredom.

18. Robert N. Ford, "Job Enrichment Lessons from AT&T," *Harvard Business Review*, 51 (January-February 1973), 96–106, outlines some very interesting examples. Also see Daniel Zwerdling, "Beyond Boredom: A Look at What's New on the Assembly Line," *Washington Monthly*, 5 (July-August 1973), 80–91.

19. There is a vast array of literature on the issue, including Likert, *The Human Organization;* Warren G. Bennis, *Changing Organizations* (New York: McGraw-Hill, 1966); Bennis and Philip E. Slater, *The Temporary Society* (New York: Harper & Row, 1968); Robert B. Blake and Jane S. Mouton, *The Managerial Grid: Key Observations for Achieving Production Through People* (Houston: Gulf, 1964); Saul W. Gellerman, *Management by Motivation* (New York: American Management Association, 1968); Gordon L. Lippitt, *Organizational Renewal: Achieving Vitality in a Changing World* (New York: Appleton-Century-Crofts, 1969).

20. For one of the most precise statements of organization development objectives, see Robert T. Golembiewski, "Organization Development in Public Agencies: Perspectives on Theory and Practice," *Public Administration Review*, 29 (July-August 1969), 367–377, especially p. 368.

21. For a detailed explanation of the approach and an example of its use, see Craig E. Schneier, Robert Pernick, and David E. Bryant, Jr., "Improving Performance in the Public Sector Through Behavior Modification and Positive Reinforcement," *Public Personnel Management*, 8 (March-April 1979), 101–110.

22. Harry Levinson, "Asinine Attitudes Towards Motivation" *Harvard*

Business Review, 51 (January-February 1973), 70–76; and Chris Argyris, "The CEO's Behavior: Key to Organizational Development," *Harvard Business Review*, 51 (March-April 1973), 55–64.

23. As defined by Nancy S. Hayward, "The Productivity Challenge," *Public Administration Review*, 36 (September-October 1976), 544–550.

24. Ibid.; and Jerome M. Rosow, "Now Is the Time for Productivity Bargaining," *Harvard Business Review*, 50 (January-February 1972), 78–89.

25. Chester A. Newland, "Personnel Concerns in Government Productivity Improvement," *Public Administration Review*, 32 (November-December 1972), 807–815, at p. 808. Raymond D. Horton, "Productivity and Productivity Bargaining in Government: A Critical Analysis," *Public Administration Review*, 36 (July-August 1976), 407–414, at pp. 409–410, takes issue with the definition on the basis that it offers few guidelines for implementation.

26. Paul D. Staudohar, "An Experiment in Increasing Productivity of Police Service Employees," *Public Administration Review*, 35 (September-October 1975), 518–522.

27. Blau, *The Dynamics of Bureaucracy*, especially chap. 3.

28. The National Center for Productivity and Quality of Working Life, *Total Performance Measurement: Some Pointers for Action* (Washington, D.C.: U.S. Government Printing Office, 1978).

29. Albert C. Hyde, "Performance Appraisal in the Post Reform Era," *Public Personnel Management*, 11 (Winter 1982), 294–305.

30. For two critiques from differing perspectives, see Douglas McGregor, "An Uneasy Look at Performance Appraisal," *Harvard Business Review*, 35 (May-June 1957), 89–94; and Douglas S. Sherwin, "The Job of Job Evaluation," *Harvard Business Review*, 35 (May-June 1957), 63–71.

31. John Nalbandian, "Performance Appraisal: If Only People Were Not Involved," *Public Administration Review*, 41 (May-June 1981), 392–396.

32. A good review of some of the legal aspects can be found in William H. Holley and Hubert S. Field, "Performance Appraisal and the Law," *Labor Law Journal*, (July 1975), 423–430.

33. Margaret A. Howell and Sidney H. Newman, "Narrative and Check-off Evaluations of Employee Performance," *Public Personnel Review*, 32 (July 1971), 148–150, presents a comparison of the validity of the two techniques and concludes that each is approximately as valid as the other.

34. Charlie B. Tyer, "Employee Performance Appraisal in American State Governments," *Public Personnel Management*, 11 (Fall 1982), 199–212.

33. Blau, *The Dynamics of Bureaucracy*, chap. 3, demonstrates the possible adverse effects of performance evaluation.

36. Arthur L. Finkle, "Can a Manager Discipline a Public Employee?" *Review of Public Personnel Administration*, 4 (Summer 1984), 83–87.

37. See Earl R. Gomersall and M. Scott Myers, "Breakthrough in On-the-Job Training," *Harvard Business Review*, 4 (July-August 1966), 62–72.

38. Leonard Greenhalgh and Robert B. McKersie, "Cost-Effectiveness of Alternative Strategies for Cut-Back Management," *Public Administration Review*, 40 (November-December 1980), 575–584.

39. Harry C. Dennis, Jr., "Reductions in Force: The Federal Experience, *Public Personnel Management* 12 (Spring 1983), 52–62; and Patricia W. Ingraham and Charles Barrilleaux, "Motivating Government Managers for Retrenchment: Some Possible Lessons from the Senior Executive Service," *Public Administration Review,* 43 (September-October 1983), 393–402.

40. For example, see William M. Timmins, "Contracting for Cooperative Personnel Services," *Public Personnel Management* 9 (1980), 196–200.

41. American Federation of State, County, and Municipal Employees, *Passing the Bucks: The Contracting Out of Public Services* (Washington, D.C.: AFSCME, 1983).

SUGGESTED READINGS

Ban, Carolyn, Edie N. Goldberg, and Toni Marzotto. "Firing the Unproductive Employee: Will Civil Service Make a Difference?" *Review of Public Personnel Administration,* 2 (Spring 1982), 87–100.

Finkle, Arthur L. "Can a Manager Discipline a Public Employee?" *Review of Public Personnel Administration,* 4 (Summer 1984), 83–87.

Flanders, Loretta R., and Rudi Klauss. "Developing Future Executives: An Assessment of Federal Efforts in an Era of Reform." *Review of Public Personnel Administration,* 2 (Spring 1982), 119–131.

Frank, Thomas M. *Resignation in Protest.* New York: Penguin, 1975.

Hyde, Albert C., and Wayne F. Cascio, eds. "Special Issue: Performance Appraisal." *Public Personnel Management,* 1 (Winter 1982), 293–375.

Klay, William Earle. "Fiscal Constraints, Trust, and the Need for a New Politics/Administration Dichotomy." *Review of Public Personnel Administration.* 4 (Fall 1983), 44–54.

Lewis, Carol W., W. Wayne Shannon, and G. Donald Ferree, Jr. "The Cutback Issue: Administrators' Perceptions, Citizen Attitudes, and Administrative Behavior." *Review of Public Personnel Administration,* 4 (Fall 1983), 12–27.

Lovrich, Nicholas P., Jr., ed. "Performance Appraisal Systems in the Public Sector: The Promise and Pitfalls of Employee Evaluation—A Symposium." *Review of Public Personnel Administration,* 3 (Summer 1983), 1–32.

Newland, Chester A., ed. "Symposium on Productivity in Government." *Public Administration Review,* 32 (November-December 1972), 739–850.

O'Toole, Daniel E., and John R. Churchill. "Implementing Pay-for-Performance: Initial Experiences." *Review of Public Personnel Administration,* 3 (Summer 1982), 13–28.

Panetta, Leon E., and Peter Gall. *Bring Us Together.* Philadelphia: Lippincott, 1971.

Rich, Wilbur C. "Bumping, Blocking and Bargaining: The Effects of Layoffs on Employees and Unions," *Review of Public Personnel Administration,* 4 (Fall 1983), 27–43.

Ronen, Simcha, and Sophia B. Primps. "The Impact of Flexitime on Performance and Attitudes in 25 Public Agencies." *Public Personnel Management*, 9 (1980), 201–207.

Saltzstein, Alan. "The Fate of Performance Appraisal: Another Death in the Bureaucracy?" *Review of Public Personnel Administration*, 3 (Summer 1983), 129–132.

Weinstein, Deena. *Bureaucratic Opposition: Challenging Abuses at the Workplace*. Elmsford, N.Y.: Pergammon, 1979.

Case 5.1: Traveling to Nowhere

Carlos O'Brien worked as a program representative in a national government agency. In order to facilitate work with grant recipients and contractors, the agency established regional offices around the country. Carlos worked out of the Kansas City office. As a program representative, he was required to travel regularly to communities within the region. His colleagues in the office had similar responsibilities. The normal procedure for travel was to submit a request and then file a travel claim within ten days of completing the travel. Once the travel request was completed, the employee could receive a travel advance for up to 75 percent of the projected travel cost. Once an advance was received, it either had to be returned, or a travel claim indicating completion of travel had to be filed within thirty days.

One day, Carlos was working in some files and came across a misplaced file that contained approved travel requests and records of travel advances for trips that were later canceled by several of his colleagues and superiors. In looking at the material, he found that many of the requests and advances were much older than thirty days; some dated almost a year back. Knowing that it was a violation of law to keep advances beyond thirty days, Carlos was concerned. He reported his findings to the agency's internal audit bureau which confirmed the violations of the law by his colleagues and superiors. They were disciplined for their actions.

Once Carlos reported what he had found, his relationships with his coworkers changed dramatically. Not surprisingly, many of them avoided him. More importantly, Carlos found that it was difficult to receive the transfers and promotions he requested and suddenly found that work no one else wanted to do was assigned to him. Finally, he was fired for incompetence after receiving an unsatisfactory performance rating two months and eight months after his report of the irregularities.

Carlos appealed to the Merit Systems Protection Board to get his job back.

INSTRUCTIONS:

You are the hearing officer for the Merit Systems Protection Board. First, write a report detailing the information you will need to decide the case. Second, make a decision based on what the information indicates. Of course, your decision will depend on the information you receive. Justify your decision according to the information you expect to obtain in your investigation and to current national government personnel policy.

Case 5.2: Chemical Dependency

Marcia Walling is faced with a delicate personnel problem. As director of the local unemployment office, she is proud of her subordinates' productivity record. She has instituted an open door policy by which employees feel free to discuss their work concerns with her, and she has made it effective through get-acquainted and organization development programs in the unit. In the year and a half she has directed the office, it has changed from one in which clients were treated as numbers to one in which employees enjoy one another and seem genuinely interested in the clientele.

But there is one problem employee. Sean Mallory was one of the best employees in the unit by all measures. In the past two months, however, he has undergone a change. Actually, he started becoming somewhat withdrawn and moody earlier than that, but everyone attributed that to his breakup with his fiancée. But instead of things getting better, they got worse. Investigating the situation, Marcia finds that Sean is often late for work and keeps clients waiting. There also are complaints from clients that he does not seem to pay attention to what is going on and that they have to repeat things or find that the information they have given is not recorded. The situation has resulted in many complaints.

Marcia decides to attempt to get to the bottom of the problem. She calls Sean in to talk with him, and he promises to mend his ways but does not wish to discuss the reasons for his work problems. Not satisfied with the interview, Marcia does some investigating on her own and finds that Sean has been involved with a social group known for its liberal use of a variety of drugs. In talking with some of Sean's coworkers, some of them indicate that Sean seems to have developed a dependency on cocaine.

INSTRUCTIONS:

You are Marcia. What should you do now? Explain your reasons.

6

Rights and Duties of Public Employees

The off-the-job conduct of public employees receives more attention than does the behavior of employees in the private sector. In its eagerness to offer high-quality public service devoid of public controversy, government often restricts the rights of those providing the service. Balancing the need for an impartial, fair, and high-quality public service with the protection of the employees' individual rights creates controversies and difficulties for public personnel systems. Of course, such problems are most likely to occur in a democratic system, in which individual rights are many and highly prized.

Restrictions on public employees' private lives have stemmed from the doctrine of privilege as applied to public employment. The courts have long held that privileges and gratuities are not subject to the same protection as rights are.[1] Thus if it is determined that something is a privilege, no one has a right to it, and such protections as due process may not apply in the same way as they would if a right were involved. Over the years the courts have held that government employment is a privilege extended to those employed and that if people want the privilege, they must abide by the conditions imposed on it. In recent years the courts have modified their stand on the issue by insisting on fair treatment in the dissemination of privileges once government decides they are to be available. Nonetheless, the privilege doctrine has been an important justification for denying public employees certain types of freedom of activity.

General Employee Conduct

Administrators in the public sector are usually forced to demand a higher standard of behavior of their employees than those in the private sector must.[2] Public employees are scrutinized by taxpayers and the media, and any misstep is likely to result in some kind of pressure for remedy. Being less dependent on the public's goodwill and facing fewer consequences from the behavior of their employees, private sector employers can be more understanding of their employees' behavior. The support of the public, and especially of the elected political leaders, is crucial to a public agency's existence. Sensitivity to the potential consequences leads many public employers to take the expedient route of restricting employee rights or imposing discipline for nonwork activities that would not be a concern in the private sector.

Police officers frequently come under special scrutiny from the community, as they are expected to be models of behavior for the rest of the citizenry. Thus it is not surprising that the city of Amarillo, Texas, dismissed a male and a female police officer in 1977 after some citizens reported that they were living together. Similarly, the city of Mesa, Arizona, dismissed a police officer with an outstanding record who decided to tell his superior officer that he was gay. Even though the department did not file any charges of his violating the law by engaging in homosexual activity, they dismissed him anyway for being gay. In both these cases, appeals to review boards and courts resulted in affirmation of the dismissals. Regardless of how one feels about the cases or issues involved, the officers were fired for behavior that is rather common, even in Amarillo and Mesa. Employees in the private sector would be much less likely to be disciplined for the same reasons. But the public clearly disapproves of its servants acting in a way that deviates from its standards and expects public employees to be models of good behavior.

In recent years, the matter of life-style has become a controversial issue in public employment. The June 1977 referendum in Dade County, Florida, epitomizes the fervor surrounding the issue. After the county commission passed an ordinance prohibiting discrimination in housing and employment against homosexuals, celebrity Anita Bryant organized a highly emotional campaign to force a referendum to repeal the ordinance. The campaign was based largely on fears that gays would be given legitimacy and the freedom to recruit children into homosexuality and on biblical quotations supposedly condemning homosexuality. The ordinance was overwhelmingly repealed by a large turnout for a special election (45 percent). The same scenario has been played out in many other places: Wichita, Kansas; Minneapolis, Minnesota; and, most recently, Houston, Texas. However, gays have been successful in some places, notably the state of California, where, in 1978, voters rejected a proposition that would have prohibited gays from being employed as teachers in the public schools. The state of Wisconsin also passed legislation prohibiting discrimination on the basis of sexual preference. Similarly, cities such as San Francisco, Los Angeles and Austin, Texas, have passed ordinances to protect the rights of gays, including the right to employment opportunity. Some actively recruit gays for their police forces.

Even as gays continue to press for protection in the hope of winning the kind of recognition given to other minorities, the controversy over the issue is not likely to abate, and it will probably be a long time before gays are generally accepted in public employment. They have few political allies, although that is changing. The issue became very visible in the 1984 election campaign, as the Democratic party ticket endorsed gay rights. This issue was also used to hurt many candidates, especially in North Carolina and Texas where the successful Republican candidates for the United States Senate used the gay support of their opponents to win over their conservative constituencies. But as gay political organizations demonstrate their political clout, they will be accorded the same consideration as other groups are, and their employment opportunities are likely to reflect that political power.

Loyalty and Security

There is probably no aspect of public personnel administration that has been more directly affected by forces in the political environment than the issues of loyalty and security. At times, officials and the public alike have reacted out of hysteria by restricting the activities of public employees. Loyalty and security are two separate concepts that are often perceived as one. Loyalty refers to the employee's support of the system, and a loyalty risk is one who would be likely consciously to subvert the political system. A security risk is someone who, without malicious intent, might divulge information or act in a way detrimental to the system. Thus someone can be a security risk without being disloyal or may be a security risk in one position but not in another.

Loyalty and freedom are competing objectives that have created numerous problems for the political system. President Washington demanded loyalty to the new federal system from his public servants, and Lincoln required loyalty to the Union. But specific tests of loyalty did not become formalized until 1939, when the Hatch Act (Section 9A) prohibited employees from being members of organizations advocating the overthrow of the government. Every period of crisis in our history, however, has produced some policies to ensure the loyalty of public servants. After World War II, the anti-Communist frenzy led to a variety of loyalty and security programs in the public service, and a number of studies of employee loyalty were conducted. For the most part, the issue attracts much less attention today, but there are still programs to protect against disloyalty. All employees of the federal government are subject to an investigation of their backgrounds to determine their suitability for the public service, although for workers in nonsensitive positions, the investigation may be conducted after placement. Those appointed to sensitive positions are investigated before appointment and are subject to more in-depth investigations. At the state and local levels, the tendency has been to require employees to sign loyalty oaths as a condition of employment, but the courts have invalidated many as being too vague and unenforceable. A 1972 Supreme Court decision did uphold the Massachusetts loyalty oath, however, and so loyalty oaths can still be used.[3]

Although it may seem reasonable that those disloyal to the system should not be employed by the government and that security risks not be employed in sensitive positions, there is little agreement on what constitutes a loyalty or security risk. Consequently, loyalty and security programs have been subject to much abuse. Many of them virtually ignore the employees' individual rights, partly because of the privilege doctrine discussed earlier.[4] Employees who are dismissed for questions of loyalty or security ordinarily can request a hearing to answer the charges.[5]

The most insidious invasion of individual rights is in regard to those applying for jobs. A person may be denied a position on the basis of background information acquired during the investigation. Whether the information is accurate may never be determined because the unsuccessful applicants are rarely told why they are unsuccessful. Thus, people may be denied jobs in the public service based on information they have no chance to see or challenge.

Political Activity Restrictions

Interest in loyalty and security programs has waned somewhat, but concern about restrictions continues to be a major contemporary issue. Such restrictions date from the English canon law tradition that certain offices or activities are inconsistent with one another.[6] Conflict-of-interest statutes, orders and rulings, and legislation or constitutional provisions prohibiting holding certain public offices concurrently are the principal methods of putting this canon law tradition into practice. The belief that politically active public servants cannot provide service free from bias led to the prohibition of certain political activities as well. In a democratic society, there may be a conflict between the rights of public employees as individuals and the right of the public to impartial service. So far in the United States, priority has been given to the public right to service, and limits have been placed on the rights of public employees as a legitimate cost for the political neutrality of the public bureaucracy.

The political activity of national government employees is restricted by the 1939 Hatch Act. In 1940 the act was amended to restrict also the political activities of state and local government employees whose salaries are paid in part or in full by federal funds. The Federal Election Campaign Act Amendments of 1974 repealed many of the restrictions on state and local government employees, although the state and local levels have their own restrictions. Before the Hatch Act was passed, the Civil Service Commission drew up a body of rules and regulations pursuant to a 1907 executive order of President Theodore Roosevelt barring activity in "political management or in political campaigns" for those covered by the civil service.[7] In implementing its rules and regulations, the commission ruled on some three thousand cases involving political activity restrictions before 1940. It is generally believed that Congress intended the Hatch Act to incorporate these decisions as established precedents for interpreting the act's political activity prohibitions. Thus Congress would effectively deny the commission the authority to interpret the legislation differently. There is some disagreement about the congressional intent, but the effect has been to hamper the flexibility of the Office of Personnel Management in dealing with the issue.[8]

Regardless of Congress's intent, the Office of Personnel Management now administers the Hatch Act and has determined that among other specific provisions, the act prohibits:

1. Serving as a delegate or alternate to a political party convention or as a member of a political committee.
2. Soliciting or handling political contributions.
3. Serving as an officer or organizer of a political club.
4. Leading or organizing political meetings or rallies or making partisan speeches to them.
5. Soliciting votes or engaging in other partisan election activity.
6. Being a candidate for a partisan political office.[9]

The rationale for such restrictions is that they will help protect public employees from being coerced into working for particular candidates or parties, that they will protect the beneficiaries of public services from such coercion, and that they will prevent public officials from using public monies and positions to further their own political careers. A more immediate political reason for the passage of the Hatch Act was a fear that the New Deal bureaucracy could be mobilized as a vast political machine in support of the administration. A similar concern among many legislators that the party in power might be able to take political advantage of politically active career servants is a major factor in Congress's reluctance to liberalize the restrictions.[10] At any rate, the Hatch Act was passed as a response to overindulgence in spoils politics, and it retains a lot of support among those who fear that unfettered spoils would return if public servants could engage in politics. Supporters of liberalization include public employee unions, but it is unlikely that they will be successful in the near future.

The constitutional rights to freedom of expression, assembly, and petition are at the heart of the controversy over the Hatch Act. Because these rights are limited by the act, many public employees argue that they are doomed to second-class citizenship.[11] In recent years a number of assaults on the Hatch Act and similar state legislation have surfaced in the courts. For a while it seemed as though the courts would invalidate many of the restrictions—as some lower courts did—but the Supreme Court, by a six-to-three decision, upheld the constitutionality of the Hatch Act and a similar state law.[12] In some places, the coverage of the restrictions has been extended, as in Arizona where the attorney general in 1983 issued an opinion that the state law even prohibited participation in nonpartisan elections. If public employees are to see a change in these restrictions, they will have to focus their efforts on legislative bodies.

The growth of collective bargaining has numerous implications for political activity. Unions could exert a great deal of pressure in the political realm if permitted to engage in partisan political activity. As a result, direct public employee organization activity in politics is usually restricted. Nonetheless, unions do support their friends through endorsements and campaigns. Collective bargaining also undermines one of the justifications for prohibiting political activity, in that it tends to reduce the likelihood that employees can be coerced or intimidated into engaging in the political activities desired by a supervisor. Because unions give workers leverage with management, employees have greater independence from their managers, and they have union support in resisting attempts by management to coerce them into political activity.

Other Restrictions

In recent years, governments have reimposed general restrictions on public employees after a period in which such restrictions were relaxed. Although the Supreme Court seems willing to permit restrictions on various aspects of an employee's personal life, it does seem to insist on procedural regulations in the imposition of such limitations. David Rosenbloom suggested that public personnel management, in its attempt to depoliticize the public service, has insisted on uniformity in public employees, with the result being a limitation on their freedom.[13] During the middle 1970s, the Court began to back away from interfering in state and local government control over personnel issues. Consequently, many jurisdictions reinstituted limitations on the freedom of expression, residency requirements, and regulations concerning appearance.[14]

Another type of restriction is that placed on "moonlighting." Prohibiting the taking of a second job, especially when combined with low salaries in many jurisdictions, may create hardships for some employees or difficulty in recruiting for the jurisdiction. The employer's concern is that an employee's ability to perform a full-time job may be affected by holding another job, and if such is the case, the employer does have a legitimate worry.

Ethics and Public Employees

Interest in public employees' ethical behavior has fluctuated greatly. Currently, Watergate and other scandals involving national leaders and some state and local governments have made ethics in the public service a central issue. And the 1984 presidential election focused attention on the issue once again because several Reagan administration officials had left office under pressure of scandal and questions were raised about the financial integrity of the Democratic vice-presidential candidate and her spouse.

One of the reasons that ethical considerations are so important to public administration is that its employees are entrusted with a great deal of discretion to decide on numerous issues that can benefit or hurt differing parties. This discretion also puts public servants under pressure to act in ways that benefit the parties affected by the agency. Public employees often find themselves on the spot, and it is up to them to decide what is right and what is wrong.

Ethical behavior is influenced by both internal individual factors and external controls. The internal factors are the degree to which individuals perceive themselves as responsible for their actions. Theoretically, employees who are carefully chosen and who embrace democratic and professional values will control their own conduct because of their dedication to the public, their professional group standards, and peer pressure.[15] Unfortunately, the pressures faced by public servants are too complex and too contradictory to allow an easy formulation of right or wrong responses. It is difficult to decide when a conflict between personal values and official duties warrants resignation or protest or whether actions such as leaking or withholding information are valid. In other words, internal controls are usually not enough.

Because internal controls are inadequate, external controls are necessary and, according to James Bowman, may be grouped into three categories: individual acts of leadership, codes of conduct, and legislation.[16] Individual leadership requires a superior who will serve as a model of behavior for his or her subordinates. Thus if the supervisor has lax standards of behavior, the subordinates can hardly be expected to maintain high standards in their performance.

Codes of conduct commonly regulate behavior, but there are differences of opinion as to their effectiveness. President Lyndon B. Johnson, for example, issued an executive order "Prescribing Standards of Ethical Conduct for Government Officers and Employees,"[17] but no mention of it was made during all of the Watergate proceedings, suggesting that no one took it very seriously. Codes of conduct provide guidelines for behavior but are often so general as to have little

meaning. Without enforcement efforts, the codes are of little value—
and enforcement is rarely pursued.

Besides identifying specific prohibited behaviors, codes of conduct
usually also require employees to avoid even the appearance of unethi-
cal behavior. Thus, something that might appear to be a conflict of
interest should be avoided. But what constitutes the appearance of a
conflict of interest poses a problem, as what seems like a conflict of
interest to some people may not appear so to others. Accepting
lunches or gifts from the people with whom one normally deals might
influence an employee's decisions or actions even if he or she insists
otherwise. And even though the individual may resist any temptation,
others may not be convinced of it. Therefore, the temptation must be
avoided to protect the integrity of the public service. Employees who
come to government from the business community often find themselves confused by these rules because behavior that is standard in
private business dealings is frowned upon or prohibited in the public
sector. It is another example of the dual standard applied to public
employees.

Because of these difficulties with codes of ethics, other methods of
prohibiting certain practices are also used. Specific legal prohibitions
on various practices are common. Most states have passed legislation
on ethical behavior for public employees in recent years, and the
Ethics in Government Act of 1978 cited specific legal prohibitions for
federal employees. It also mandated the Office of Personnel Management to spell out specific rules and regulations implementing the act
and established an Office of Government Ethics within the OPM.

The national law is controversial. It requires employees above the
GS-16 level to disclose their financial interests and prohibits the employment of federal employees by private sector firms dealing with
their agencies for two years after the employee leaves the public service. Furthermore, employees are restricted from representing others
before their former government employer agency or from influencing
that agency. Many officials are concerned that these restrictions deter
competent people from seeking public sector jobs, and the broadness
of the statute has caused employees to petition Congress to change the
law. But given the constant scandals involving the questionable behavior of many Reagan adminstration appointees, the effectiveness of the
statute is debatable.

The difficulties with the federal law illustrate the problems in
attempting to ensure the integrity of public employees. Obviously,

government expects its employees not to use their positions for their personal gain. The questions are how far government should go in controlling its employees' behavior and what serves the public interest.

Nondiscriminatory Work Place

The right not to be discriminated against has become a major issue in public employee rights. The 1972 Equal Employment Opportunity Act extended coverage of the 1964 Civil Rights Act to state and local governments. Much litigation has arisen from discrimination or perceived discrimination by public employers, and governments have been required to take compensatory action when they have been found to be discriminating in employment practices. This issue will be discussed in the next chapter.

An issue that arises from the nondiscrimination policy now prevalent in public employment is sexual harassment. Because the work place is changing with respect to sexual composition, sexual harassment has also become a major concern of organizations. Sexual harassment refers to an environment in the organization that allows sexual innuendos, solicitation of sexual favors, and personnel decisions conditioned on submitting to sexual advances. Clearly, the last item is acknowledged to be sexual harassment, but other forms of sexual harassment are not as readily agreed upon. Nonetheless, the courts have dealt with the issue increasingly in the past decade, and the definition has been broadened to include any unwanted sexual suggestions or actions.[18]

The extent of sexual harassment is just becoming clear. The national government conducted a survey in 1980 that showed surprising results.[19] Nearly one-fourth of federal employees reported some form of sexual harassment, with female employees reporting such concerns much more frequently than males did. There is no reason to believe that the situation is any different in state and local governments. Many employees are vulnerable, and harassment may be used to coerce them into untenable situations. Furthermore, employers may find themselves the objects of lawsuits if they do not protect their employees from sexual harassment. Therefore, guidelines are being drawn up for employees so that they will not engage in such harassment. If employers take steps to prevent harassment and respond quickly to complaints of it, they may avoid liability. This quick response should be an investigation of the complaint and appropriate remedial action. The employer cannot retaliate against the employee rather than correct the action, as was common in the past.

Grievance Procedures and Appeals

When employees feel that they have been wronged, they need a fair and speedy system for examining and resolving their complaint. Now with collective bargaining, a grievance procedure is normally negotiated in the bargaining agreement. Provision is made for an outside neutral party to decide on the complaint. Normally, each party is committed to accepting the neutral party's decision. Such a system is usually referred to as grievance arbitration.

Because of the threat of unionization and because courts usually insist on procedural regularities in dealing with employees' complaints and discipline, many employers have devised grievance systems of their own.[20] A grievance procedure spells out the situation in which employees may seek redress of a grievance, provides steps for processing the grievance, specifies the time limits in which action must be taken, and provides for a final decision. In most systems, informal resolution is encouraged. The subordinate is supposed to work out the problem with the immediate supervisor. If the problem remains unsolved, formal grievance procedures will be followed.

Ronald L. Miller found in his survey of one thousand public and private employers that there are five basic models of grievance procedure systems for nonunion employees.[21] The models are differentiated primarily on whether external review is available and on who makes the final decision. The first model provides for grievances on any issue and allows for several review steps within the organization. The organization's chief administrator makes the final decision on the grievance; thus employees have no access to an outside neutral review. The second model is a variation of the first except that after the internal review, a neutral party is used in an advisory capacity. The advice of the neutral party may go to the chief administrator or possibly to an outside arbitrator, depending on the issues.

The third model permits grievances on only a certain number of issues. Sometimes issues such as suspension or dismissal cases are given a single internal review, whereas other issues are appealed through several internal steps. Then the case goes to a neutral third party and finally the chief administrator; again, the management is the final judge. The fourth model has cases go through an internal review process to a neutral third party and then to arbitration, thus paralleling most negotiated grievance procedures. The last model permits internal review, after which cases go directly to a governing board such as a civil service commission or to the chief executive officer.

The first model, in which virtually anything can be grieved and management monitors itself, was found to be most common. Such a system provides little support for the employee; instead, employees are likely to be suspicious of the system. Even if the employee's complaint is upheld, morale in the organization will be damaged as management adjudges one of its own to be deficient in supervision.[22] Supervisors are the ones who feel uncomfortable with the system's using a neutral third party. The organization has the unenviable task of balancing the employees' concern about the system's credibility with the supervisors' need for the organization's support.

The Civil Service Reform Act of 1978 streamlined the national government's grievance and appeals process for those not covered by negotiated grievance procedures. In agencies without negotiated procedures, the employees may appeal adverse actions (removals, suspensions, reductions in grade or pay) to the Merit Systems Protection Board (MSPB). If the board rules against the agency, the agency may be required to pay the fee of the employee's attorney.

In cases of alleged discrimination, the appeal of agency action may go to the Equal Employment Opportunity Commission (EEOC). If the case involves issues over which the MSPB has jurisdiction and it also includes discrimination complaints, the case will be decided by the MSPB and reviewed by the EEOC.

Employees can usually appeal to the courts if they are not satisfied with the results of the normal appeals process. But a court review is rarely a realistic alternative because of the crowded dockets and high costs of court relief. Nonetheless, the courts are stepping into such cases and are insisting that due process be followed in personnel matters.

Management often perceives grievance procedures as something available to employees to buck the will of management; however, they do have a number of positive effects as well.[23] One of the most important has been the recognition that supervisory training is a significant need in many organizations. In addition, grievance procedures may help bring about solid collective bargaining procedures, correct detrimental agency practices, develop equitable methods of dealing with employees, ensure accountability, and lead to further evaluation and modification of the grievance mechanism itself.

Summary

Employees obviously have certain duties and responsibilities as members of the public service, but they also have rights as citizens. Balancing these rights with the expectations of supervisors and the public is a difficult task. Management and the public expect public employees to be models for the rest of society. As a result, public employees are often subjected to different standards of behavior than are other citizens. They are often called upon to refrain from activities such as political activities that citizens take for granted. At the same time, many pressures can be exerted on employees by their managers and supervisors; thus, protections from such coercion are also elements of public personnel policy.

NOTES

1. For a complete explanation of the privilege doctrine and its implications, see Kenneth Culp Davis, *Administrative Law Text*, 3rd ed. (St. Paul: West Publishing, 1972), pp. 175–189.

2. W. D. Heisel and Richard M. Gladstone, "Off-the-Job Conduct As a Disciplinary Problem," *Public Personnel Review*, 28 (January 1968), 23–28, presents an interesting study of the issue. For a case study, see Peter Schuck, "The Curious Case of the Indicted Meat Inspectors," *Harper's*, September 1972, pp. 81–88.

3. *Cole v Richardson*, 403 U.S. 917 (1972).

4. See the Supreme Court decisions in *Bailey v Richardson*, 341 U.S. 918 (1951); and *Greene v McElroy*, 360 U.S. 474 (1959), for divergent rulings on the issue.

5. Of course, during periods of hysteria such as the 1950s, hearings may not be available, and even if they are, they can become abuses in themselves. For a variety of perspectives, see Hans J. Morgenthau, "The Impact of the Loyalty and Security Measures on the State Department," *Bulletin of the Atomic Scientists*, 11 (April 1955), 134–140; Bar of the City of New York, *Report of the Special Committee on the Federal Loyalty Security Program* (New York: Dodd, Mead, 1956); and Earl Latham, *The Communist Controversy in Washington: From the New Deal to McCarthy* (Cambridge, Mass.: Harvard University Press, 1966).

6. Otto Kirchheimer, "The Historical and Comparative Background of the Hatch Act," *Public Policy*, 2 (1941), 341–373, presents an outstanding analysis of the history and philosophy behind the restrictions on political activity. Another good source is by H. Eliot Kaplan, "Political Neutrality of the Public Service," *Public Personnel Review*, 1 (1940), 10–23.

7. Executive Order 642, June 3, 1907.

8. Henry Rose, "A Critical Look at the Hatch Act," *Harvard Law Review*, 75 (January 1962), 510–526, reviews the congressional debate and intent as well as differing opinions.

9. As outlined by United States Civil Service Commission Pamphlet No. 20, *Political Activities of Federal Officers and Employees* (Washington, D.C.: U.S. Government Printing Office, May 1966).

10. See Philip L. Martin, "The Hatch Act in Court: Some Recent Developments," *Public Administration Review*, 33 (September-October 1973), 443–447; and David H. Rosenbloom, "The Sources of Continuing Conflict Between the Constitution and Public Personnel Management," *Review of Public Personnel Administration*, 2 (Fall 1981), 3–18.

11. Philip L. Martin, "The Constitutionality of the Hatch Act: Second-Class Citizenship for Public Employees," *University of Toledo Law Review*, 6 (Fall 1974), 78–109.

12. In *U.S. Civil Service Commission* v *National Association of Letter Carriers*, 93 S.Ct. 2880 (1973). Also see Martin, "The Hatch Act in Court," for an analysis of this and other relevant decisions.

13. Rosenbloom, "The Sources of Continuing Conflict."

14. See *Kelly* v *Johnson*, 425 U.S. 238 (1976), in which the Supreme Court ruled that grooming regulations for police officers were legitimate, in that the Constitution does not guarantee the right of police officers to choose their own life-style when it can affect their jobs. *McCarthy* v *Philadelphia*, 96 U.S. 1154 (1976), sanctioned residency requirements.

15. Carl J. Friedrich, "Public Policy and the Nature of Administrative Responsibility," *Public Policy*, 1940, pp. 3–24, presents the case for professional and peer group control.

16. James S. Bowman, "Ethics in the Federal Service: A Post-Watergate View," *Midwest Review of Public Administration*, 11 (March 1977), 3–20. Herman Finer, "Administrative Responsibility in Democratic Government," *Public Administration Review*, 1 (1941), 335–350, presents the argument for the formal legal controls.

17. Executive Order 11222, May 8, 1965.

18. Important decisions include *Tompkins* v *Public Service Electric and Gas Company*, 422 Supp. 533 (1977); and *Bundy* v *Jackson* 24 EDP 31439 (1981).

19. Merit Systems Protection Board, *Sexual Harassment in the Federal Workplace: Is It a Problem?* (Washington, D.C.: U.S. Government Printing Office, 1981).

20. Philip L. Martin, "The Improper Discharge of a Federal Employee by a Constitutionally Permissible Process: The OEO Case," *Administrative Law Review*, 28 (Winter 1976), 27–39; and Richard L. Epstein, "The Griev-

130   *Public Personnel Administration in the United States*

ance Procedure in the Nonunion Setting: Caveat Employer," *SPEER Newsletter* (Special Supplement, February 1978), 1–4.
  21. Ronald L. Miller, "Grievance Procedures for Nonunion Employees," *Public Personnel Management*, 7 (September-October 1978), 302–311.
  22. Epstein, "The Grievance Procedure."
  23. Joseph Shane, "Indirect Functions of the Grievance Procedure," *Public Personnel Management*, 2 (May-June 1973), 171–178.

SUGGESTED READINGS

Bolton, John R. *The Hatch Act: A Civil Libertarian Defense*. Washington, D.C.: American Enterprise Institute for Policy Research, 1976.
Donahue, Robert J. "Disciplinary Actions in New York State Service: A Radical Change." *Public Personnel Management*, 4 (March-April 1975), 110–112.
Dworkin, Robert P. *Rights of the Public Employee*. Chicago: American Library Association, 1978.
Martin, Philip L. "The Hatch Act in Court: Some Recent Developments." *Public Administration Review*, 33 (September-October 1973), 443–447.
———. "Return to the Privilege-Right Doctrine in Public Employment." *Labor Law Journal*, (June 1977), 361–368.
Neugarten, Dail A., and Jay M. Shafritz, eds. *Sexuality in Organizations: Romantic and Coercive Behaviors at Work*. Oak Park, Ill.: Moore Publishing, 1980.
Rose, Henry. "A Critical Look at the Hatch Act." *Harvard Law Review*, 75 (January 1962), 510–526.
Rosenbloom, David H. "The Constitution and the Civil Service: Some Recent Developments, Judicial and Political," *Kansas Law Review*, 18 (June 1970), 839–869.
———. "The Sources of Continuing Conflict Between the Constitution and Public Personnel Management." *Review of Public Personnel Administration*, 2 (Fall 1981), 3–18.
Tidwell, Gary L. "Employment at Will: Limitations in the Public Sector." *Public Personnel Management*, 13 (Fall 1984), 293–305.
Timmins, William. *Long Hair in a Merit System: An Appeal from Utopia Avenue*. Syracuse, N.Y.: Inter-University Case Program, 1972.

Case 6.1: The Embattled Union Leader

Cory Paul has been president of the state Public Labor Council for fifteeen years. During that time, he has been on leave from his job at the Department of Transportation. The 1984 gubernatorial election was a very spirited one, with the Republican incumbent eventually winning. Because the incumbent had been very antilabor in her first administration, the Public Labor Council, at Paul's urging, endorsed and worked for the election of the Democratic candidate. There was nothing unusual about the activity, as the council had done the same during its fifty-year history in the state.

Three months after the election, Cory Paul received a certified letter from the state personnel director. The letter informed him that he had violated the state's little "Hatch Act" which prohibits political activity by state employees. Specifically, Cory was charged with endorsing and campaigning for the election of the Democratic nominee for governor, contrary to the provisions of the law that had been in effect for twenty-five years.

Cory was angry and confused. In his fifteen years as president of the Public Labor Council he could not remember such a thing happening. In fact, no such case had occurred during the entire history of the little Hatch Act.

The options for Cory were rather limited. The letter informed him that he would be prosecuted for violating the law and be given punishment ranging from suspension to termination. He was also offered the opportunity to resign instead, in which case the charges would be dropped.

Cory decided that he would fight the charges and filed an appeal with the Personnel Appeals Board which handles disputes over personnel actions. His appeal requested that the charges be dismissed and that his record be expunged of any reference to the charges against him.

INSTRUCTIONS:

You are the hearing examiner. What will you want to know? On the basis of the information you are likely to receive, what will be your decision and the reasons for it?

Case 6.2: Rosa's Dilemma

Rosa Castaneda works for the city office of information management and is in charge of purchasing new equipment and developing training in the use of new technology, among other duties. Her immediate superior is the director of the office. The director introduced Rosa to Marcy Long, who is a training consultant. Marcy and the director have been long-time friends, and Marcy is just beginning her own consulting business. The director, John Hale, made clear to Rosa that if possible, he would like the office to give Marcy a contract for training.

Rosa did not think anymore about it until one day she received a request from John to approve a consulting contract with Marcy to develop a training system for an integrated information software system. John indicated that he would like to improve the agency staff's ability to share information and that Marcy had just the program to do it. The cost of the training project was $7,450. Rosa felt that even though bids were not required for contracts under $7,500, she should discuss it with John. She felt that the department should draw up a request for proposals for the project and permit others to bid on it. But John told her to go ahead and approve the contract with Marcy. Rosa did so.

The training program seemed to be a good one, although there was no evaluation of its impact. Again, John Hale came to Rosa Castaneda and asked her to approve more training contracts with Marcy Long. This time there were three separate contracts, two for $3,500 each and one for $5,400. Rosa told John that she would not sign the contracts because she felt that they violated the spirit, if not the letter, of the law. Hale then told her to sign the contracts or she would be fired.

INSTRUCTIONS:

You are Rosa Castaneda. What do you do? Explain the reasons for your actions.

7

Labor-Management Relations

There are many differences between public and private sector personnel management, but none is more clear-cut than the differences in collective bargaining. Whereas the private sector has had a long history of collective bargaining, the public sector did not have effective collective bargaining until the 1960s. The term *labor-management relations* is preferred by many public managers as an indication of government's reluctant acceptance of bargaining. Labor-management relations actually refers to all aspects of the interchange between labor and management, and collective bargaining refers more specifically to the process by which labor and management participate in mutual decision making regarding the work situation. In such decision making, employees organize and select a representative to work with management on their behalf. In the absence of collective bargaining, employees are on their own and must negotiate individually with their employers.

Although much of the growth in public sector collective bargaining has been recent, some public employees have a long history of unionization. Craftsmen in naval installations, for example, have been organized since the early part of the nineteenth century, and the National Association of Letter Carriers came into existence in the late nineteenth century as an affiliate of the American Federation of Labor. Some state and local employees have also been unionized for a relatively long period of time. The International Association of Fire Fighters, an AFL-CIO affiliate, started in the 1880s as local social clubs and fire fighters' benefit societies. Similarly, the American Federation of State, County, and Municipal Employees (AFSCME) began in 1936 under the auspices of the American Federation of Labor. The American Federation of Labor (AFL) and the Congress of Industrial Organizations (CIO) were national umbrella organizations that provided financial, political, and technical support to individual affiliates and local organizations. Originally one organization, they split in 1937 over internal disagreements about approaches to collective bargaining and because of personality conflicts among some of the leaders. After many years of spirited competition, the two groups merged again in 1955 to form the AFL-CIO.

Unionization, however, does not necessarily entail collective bargaining. It was not until the 1960s that collective bargaining played an important part in public personnel administration.[1] President John Kennedy's Executive Order 10988 in 1962 was a major force in stimulating public sector bargaining activity. It granted federal employees the right to organize and engage in collective bargaining. Executive Orders 11491 (1969) and 11616 (1971) by President Richard Nixon and 11838 (1975) by President Gerald Ford clarified and formalized the bargaining process for federal employees. The Civil Service Reform Act of 1978 brought about further changes, which will be discussed later in the chapter. One of the most significant features of the reform act was to spell out in statute the right to collective bargaining, so that presidents would no longer have the authority to regulate the process on their own. The process by which personnel decisions are made reflects the influence of labor organizations since the early 1960s.

Government Resistance

Several factors account for the lack of public sector collective bargaining in the past. Among them were an unfavorable legal environment, legal doctrines of government sovereignty and privilege, an essentiality-of-services argument, the professional status of many public employees, the pay and fringe benefit levels of some employees, and the availability of other means by which employees could attain their objectives. In addition, the public's negative reaction to collective bargaining among government employees slowed the process' development.

The current political environment is one in which unions enjoy little public support. The 1960s and 1970s were unusual in that public opinion tended to support public employee unions and bargaining. Otherwise, the general public has been suspicious of the prospects and potential effects of bargaining activities. Many are afraid that unions already have too much power and would only gain more if they were permitted to bargain with the government. Because unions help elect the public officials who are supposed to represent the public, many critics feel that public employees would enjoy an undue advantage if they also had unions bargaining for them.[2]

The power of unions may be exaggerated. Public employee unions, especially at the federal level, are restricted from engaging in partisan political activity and cannot negotiate for union security agreements guaranteeing that the employees they represent will join the union or pay dues.[3] There are also numerous restrictions on what items can be bargained: pay and fringe benefits are excluded in federal bargaining and in some state and local jurisdictions. As some writers have pointed out, public employee unions are also at a disadvantage because they have no natural allies in the political process, as most organized political interests find them easy targets for attack.[4] Management often uses the fear of union power to justify denying collective bargaining to public employees.

The political climate also contributed to a legal framework in which bargaining was made difficult. Government employees were specifically exempted from the protections of the Wagner and Taft-Hartley acts, which spelled out the rights and responsibilities of parties in private sector bargaining. Also, before 1960 the courts consistently held that public employees had no constitutional right to join or organize unions, and public employers were under no obligation to bargain with employees. Starting in 1954, when by executive order, Mayor Robert Wagner granted New York City employees the right to organize, the legal environment underwent rapid change. The collective bargaining apparatus was established in 1958, and the city began its bargaining process. In 1959 Wisconsin became the first state to authorize collective bargaining for public employees; however, only local government employees were affected, as state employees were exempted from the law. But with the aforementioned Kennedy order, the 1960s saw a flourishing of unionization and bargaining at all levels of government.

Before the Kennedy order, collective bargaining was nonexistent in the federal government service, although the Lloyd-LaFollette Act of 1912 granted employees the right to join labor organizations and to petition Congress without fear of reprisal. Before passage of that act, federal employees were subject to mandatory discharge and forfeiture of civil service status for union activity. Similarly, legislation in 1955 declared that a strike against the federal government was a felony and disqualified the participant from federal employment. The Kennedy executive order, however, signaled a turning point in labor relations. As it changed federal policy on bargaining with federal government employees, it also stimulated state and local governments to reexamine and change many of their policies.

There is no common legal framework under which state and local government relations are governed. The fifty states have their own policies or nonpolicies, and many other variations exist in the approximately eighty thousand local government jurisdictions across the country. Labor relations take place under policies made through common law doctrine, judicial decisions, executive orders, statutes, ordinances, and attorneys general opinions.

Some forty-five states have statutes that govern collective bargaining among public employees, but there the similarity ends. States such as Michigan, Indiana, New York, and Hawaii have comprehensive laws covering all public employees. Other states such as Texas and Georgia have legislation governing certain groups of employees, such as police, fire fighters, and teachers. Still others—for example, North Carolina and Tennessee—prohibit state and local entities from bargaining with their employees. Finally, in the absence of legislation in some states— Arizona, Arkansas, and Virginia among them—policy has been established by court decisions or the opinions of the attorney general. Only Mississippi has no stated policy on the issue.[5]

The sovereignty of government doctrine has been used to preclude public employees from bargaining. This concept holds that government is the agent of the people and cannot delegate authority to others, such as employee organizations, without violating the people's trust. In other words, the authority is not the government's to delegate. In recent years the doctrine has waned in significance, as governments have found it necessary to delegate power in a variety of areas and as the courts have weakened the doctrine in many of its decisions.[6]

The privilege doctrine is another legal device that has been used to discourage public sector collective bargaining. This doctrine holds that some of the benefits that governments confer are privileges and not rights. For example, education, welfare, and the like have been adjudged to be privileges. Similarly, public employment is viewed as a privilege extended to employees by government. Government can restrict that privilege, and the prohibition of collective bargaining was one such restriction. But as with the sovereignty doctrine, the courts have greatly modified the privilege doctrine and it no longer restricts bargaining in the public sector.[7]

Services performed by governments have ordinarily been characterized as essential, and bargaining has been denied to public employees because of this essentiality of services. Particularly because collective bargaining is often equated with strikes, the prohibition of bargaining has been justified as a way of preventing the interruption of services. This argument has been weakened as of late because many of the services that government provides are not viewed as essential. In fact, many private sector services—the telephone, for example—would be more difficult to do without than would many government services such as education or highway maintenance. Furthermore, experience with the loss of services, such as sanitation, police, and education, through strikes has demonstrated that people can cope with the situation for a limited time and has lessened the fears surrounding collective bargaining.

Even public employees themselves have often been hesitant to engage in collective bargaining. Until the 1960s, unions and other labor organizations were not held in high esteem by public employees. Much public sector labor is white-collar, and there has been a tendency for employees to think of labor organizations as typically blue-collar. Teachers, in particular, have been split over whether it is professional to belong to a union and engage in collective bargaining. But finding that unions could bring them gains, public employees have been changing their views, and many professional associations are becoming bargaining agents for public employees.

Although the pay and benefits of state and local government employees are often poor, federal employees have very good benefits. Compensation, though not excessive, has also been relatively good at the starting and middle levels of the federal service. As a result, federal employees did not see as much of a need for collective bargaining as some of their counterparts did. Nonetheless, federal workers are now more highly unionized than is any other governmental sector: approximately 60 percent of eligible employees are union members.

Finally, public employees have sometimes been slow to organize because they have other means at their disposal for gaining their objectives. Because the decision makers are elected politicians, they pay attention to blocks of voters, and public employees often constitute a major block. And because legislative bodies often retain control over public employees' pay and benefits, lobbying is also an important method for gaining influence. The lack of centralized authority in the political system also permits interests to gain in one place what they could not get in another. Thus if the executive does not satisfy the group, the group can go to the legislative body or a competing board or agency. Public employee groups have been effective in taking advantage of these fragmented political structures, particularly at the local level.

Politics and Bargaining

Most experts agree that the main factor that differentiates public and private sector collective bargaining is the political nature of the decision-making process in public sector bargaining.[8] As Theodore Clark observed, collective bargaining is premised on the idea that the two parties to the bargaining process are adversaries who seek their own interests and that each party selects its representative without being influenced by the other party.[9] In the public sector, however, political considerations serve to violate these premises. In particular, public employee organizations participate in the selection of management through involvement in interest group politics and through the election process. In short, employee organizations have special access to the management's decision-making process, thus enhancing the organizations' power vis à vis management. Much of the literature on public sector bargaining decries the special position enjoyed by the public employee labor organizations and suggests that unions and the like dominate the process as a result.[10]

Summers, on the other hand, believes that public employees need that special access because they face formidable opposition from all other interests in the political process.[11] Because tax revenues have to be raised or levels of service reduced to finance public employee demands, the political opposition to employee demands can be intense. The taxpayer revolts symbolized by California's Proposition 13 in 1978 and its stimulation of similar efforts in other jurisdictions attest to the impact that an aroused electorate can have. Similarly, public employees in San Francisco bore the brunt of taxpayer discontent with some of the employees' gains in 1974 and 1975. Through referenda, salaries were rolled back, and limits were established regarding how and what could be bargained. Thus, abuses by employee unions can be cited, but active citizen participation in the political process can also dwarf the influence of public employee organizations.

The political nature of public sector bargaining is also reflected in the way management selects its representatives and decides on the policy it will bring to the bargaining table. Again, as Summers pointed out, citizens have an interest in these issues, whereas in the private sector, management makes such decisions without public involvement.[12] Because decisions on how management will select a representative and on what the bargaining position will be are matters of public concern, employee organizations can participate in them, again augmenting their influence. On the other hand, management is normally prohibited from attempting to influence the employees' selection of bargaining agents and positions.

It is also difficult for management to send someone to the bargaining table who can bind public management. There are many other decision makers to whom the employee organizations can appeal if they do not get satisfaction in the actual bargaining process. Many times city councils or other legislative bodies need to ratify agreements and are hesitant to give up any authority to change elements of the agreement. Similarly, legislative bodies retain control over many aspects of the work situation, either mandating or setting restrictions on personnel practices. For local governments, the issue is even more complicated by the fact that state legislation can mandate practices for all governmental bodies. If a state minimum salary or other requirement is imposed, the local jurisdiction will have little flexibility. This is because the costs normally have to be borne by the local government, even though the policy comes from above. Public employee organizations use their access to elected political leaders to influence decision-making processes and participate in the election of such officials.

Another political aspect of public sector collective bargaining is that personnel issues have larger policy implications. They are part of the policymaking process to the extent that the political representatives make the decisions in many cases and affect such issues as tax policy, budgeting, and level of services. The political representatives are influenced by what will gain them votes. Such concerns often lead to problems if the political leader does not own up to the consequences of trying to curry favor with employee organizations for the purpose of gaining elective office. Officials in some cities, such as New York City, have agreed to contracts whose costs will be borne by future administrations. Pension plans in particular are often subject to such political manipulation. In the short run, the politician gains, but the taxpayers and succeeding officials are then faced with bearing the long-term cost. Unless the public is made fully aware of the ultimate cost, it is difficult to prevent opportunistic politicians from taking advantage of the situation.

Because of these problems, the "fish bowl" approach to public sector bargaining has many advocates. The fish bowl approach means that the bargaining is done in public. In the private sector, closed door sessions are almost universal. The public sector, however, runs into problems when it conducts closed negotiation sessions: in a democratic society, people are supposed to know what is going on so that they can retain control over the system. If bargaining is conducted in private, they cannot participate in the process, and hence they must relinquish control to those who do participate in the negotiation. On the other hand, when negotiation takes place in open meetings, participants may find themselves pushed into corners on issues. Once people state a position publicly, it becomes difficult to change it because they may be perceived as backing down. Because negotiation requires compromise, it becomes exceedingly difficult to bargain effectively in public sessions. There is no easy way of reconciling the need for openness in democratic government and the need for frankness and compromise in collective bargaining.

Elements of a Labor Relations System

A public labor management relations system is created by public policy, whether it be in the form of legislation, executive order, court decision, or legal opinion. The policy normally provides for basic rules and steps in the bargaining process. Of course, the question of whether the right to bargain is to exist is the system's most basic element.

ADMINISTRATION OF LABOR-MANAGEMENT RELATIONS

If the right to bargain is granted, there must be some way to administer the process; thus, most policies assign the responsibility to an existing agency or create a new one. The national government, under the Civil Service Reform Act of 1978, created the Federal Labor Relations Authority (FLRA) to oversee bargaining unit determination, supervise elections, and coordinate agency labor management activities. The FLRA consists of three bipartisan presidential appointees, with one designated as the chairperson. Also appointed is a general counsel who investigates unfair labor practices, and the Federal Service Impasses Panel resolves impasses in negotiation. At the state and local levels, the supervision of the collective bargaining process is varied. Some states create an agency whose sole purpose is to supervise public employee labor relations—usually including local governments. Maine, New York, and Hawaii are examples of such states. Another approach is to assign the responsibility to personnel departments, departments of labor, or personnel boards, as is done in Alaska, Massachusetts, Montana, and Wisconsin. A combination of approaches may also be used, in which a state board may oversee collective bargaining generally but individual departments have the specific responsibility for bargaining in their areas. Thus it is common to see departments of education or local boards of education having responsibility for supervising their own bargaining.

UNIT DETERMINATION

Unit determination refers to those employees who will be considered as a unit for bargaining purposes. The criteria for making such a decision are community of interest, desires of the employees and employer, history of experience, efficiency of management, and limiting fragmentation. Community of interest pertains to the similarities of the people in the proposed unit. Similarity of duties, skills, and working conditions, job classifications, employee benefits, common promotional ladders, and common supervision are some of the factors considered. In addition, employees may be grouped together because of the amount of interchange, integration of physical operations, or centralization of administrative and managerial functions. The main concern is having a bargaining unit consisting of employees who have similar interests so that they can work together.

Employees often like to have many units because the narrower the group's interests are, the greater its solidarity is likely to be. Sometimes that concern is sacrificed for size, though, as too-narrow a focus may lead to very small numbers of eligible employees for the unit. Management usually prefers larger units because there are likely to be disagreements within the unit and also because when the unit is large, it can deal with fewer representatives.

The two main types of units are agency and occupational. Agency units are those in which a particular department or agency is the basis for organizing the bargaining process. The Treasury Department at the national level and police and fire departments at the local levels are examples of agency units. The state of Minnesota uses agency units throughout the state service. An advantage for management is that the channels of communication are already in place in the agencies. However, there may be problems with inequity among similar employees in different units, and consensus is often difficult to achieve because so many types of employees may be employed in the same agency.

Occupational units are based on the type of work done. Thus, all clerical staff may be in the same unit, all lab technicians in another, and so on. Clearly, each group is likely to have well-defined interests, and similar work in different agencies will be covered under similar policies. Managers often have difficulty with this approach because it centralizes authority on bargained issues, thus weakening departmental control over employees.

Some jurisdictions use a combination of the two approaches. New York City, for example, bargains over some issues (like overtime, RIF policies, grievance procedures) citywide. Other issues, such as case loads, may be bargained at departmental levels, and still others related to items like salary for particular job titles may be bargained at yet another designated level. Such a system is said to have multilevel units.

One issue that comes up in the public sector but not in the private sector is whether supervisors should be in the same unit with the people they supervise. In the private sector, supervisors generally are not permitted to bargain, and if they are, they are in separate units. In the public sector, it is not uncommon to find supervisors in the same units with their subordinates. Police and fire departments often have everyone except the chief in their bargaining unit. Conflicts can arise because the bargaining unit representative has to represent the employee in grievances. If the supervisor against whom the grievance is made is also a member of the unit, there will be a conflict of interest. The steward is supposed to represent everyone in the unit and certainly cannot represent both sides at the same time. Being in the bargaining unit with subordinates also compromises the supervisor's role as a member of the management team. In the public sector, these problems arise because the role of supervisors is not as clear as it is in the private sector. Supervisors in the public sector are often considered lead workers in their units but are not considered part of management. Thus there is confusion over whether they should be part of the bargaining unit.

BARGAINING REPRESENTATIVES

Management often has difficulty organizing for bargaining because of the fragmentation of political authority in government units. Nonetheless, as bargaining activity has increased, most jurisdictions with much bargaining have hired labor relations experts to lead negotiations and administer the overall labor-management relations program. Working with the labor relations expert will usually be representatives of personnel, legal counsel, and representatives of the department or unit to which negotiations pertain.

Employees choose representatives to bargain for them. The selection process usually requires an election in which employees decide whether to adopt collective bargaining and, if so, who will bargain for them. The election of who will represent the unit is known as the certification election, and like the election on whether to bargain at all, it is supervised by the agency with responsibility for administering the labor-management relations program. The two actions may be taken at the same or in separate elections. Representatives of employees fall into three main categories: unions, employee associations, and professional associations.

Unions, of course, are the most readily recognized participants in collective bargaining, as they have been the traditional agents of employees in the private sector. Unions in the public sector may have only public employee members or be mixed membership unions; that is, have members from both the public and private sectors. The largest public sector union is the American Federation of State, County, and Municipal Employees (AFSCME) with a membership of approximately 1 million. Membership tells only part of the story, however. Unions in the public sector represent everyone in the bargaining unit, even though they cannot require all employees in the unit to be dues-paying members. Thus AFSCME represents well over 1.5 million employees at local, state, and national levels.

Representing mostly federal government employees are three other relatively large unions. The American Federation of Government Employees (AFGE) represents approximately 700,000 employees and has about 270,000 members, and the National Federation of Federal Employees (NFFE) represents 136,000 and has about 35,000 members. The National Treasury Employees Union (NTEU) represents about 110,000 and has about 70,000 members. Many public employee unions, like their private sector counterparts, are having difficulty retaining members. One reason given for the loss of members is that employees do not believe that unions and collective bargaining can help on the most important issues of wages and benefits. Working conditions have improved to the point that many employees no longer see the need for unions to protect their interests. Taken for granted are relatively safe working conditions and programs to protect employee security in times of illness and injury. Without a strong perceived need for their services, unions have to convince employees of their benefits, and with their current image, that is not always an easy job.

The uniformed services are represented by unions with an almost exclusively public sector membership. Police are represented by two major organizations, the Fraternal Order of Police (FOP) and the International Conference of Police Associations (ICPA). Some other unions such as AFSCME and the Teamsters also represent the police in some jurisdictions. Because police protection is one of those essential services that people are afraid of losing, these unions have usually been successful in obtaining their demands. Police unions usually play up the professional nature of their work and organizations rather than the union image that normally goes with such employee organizations. Sick-ins and slowdowns are common techniques used by police employee unions.

When strikes do occur, the current political climate dampens the public's enthusiasm for them. And strikes are not always successful, as the experience of the New Orleans police in 1979 demonstrated. The strike, timed to occur during Mardi Gras, the city's busiest tourist season, was calculated to bring the pressure of business and the community to bear on the public officials. The union expected that such pressure would make management settle quickly, to the benefit of the police. The actual result was that much of the Mardi Gras celebration was curtailed; the police union lost its credibility with, and the support of, the community; and management held out until the police were willing to settle for what was essentially management's original offer. The New Orleans experience demonstrates the taxpayers' growing frustration and shows that unions do not necessarily always get what they want. Similarly, President Reagan's firing of 11,500 air traffic controllers who went out on strike in 1981 was a dramatic message to public employees that strikes could be broken. This action encouraged many public employers to take harder lines with their employee representatives.

Fire fighters also have a long tradition of collective bargaining in an essential service. They are almost unique among public employees, because the International Association of Fire Fighters (IAFF) exercises virtually exclusive jurisdiction over them. In contrast with the police organizations, the 170,000-member IAFF has traditionally stressed its union image and is associated with the AFL-CIO. Although the national union does not officially sanction strikes, it does provide assistance to striking locals.

As noted earlier, some unions consist of membership from both the public and the private sectors. During the late 1950s many private sector unions lost members, and looked to the growing public sector to increase their rolls. These unions usually seek members from all levels of government rather than from just one level. The AFL-CIO now has a department devoted entirely to public sector collective bargaining. Reflecting the private sector's tradition, these unions tend to be more occupationally segregated and more likely to favor strikes. Among these mixed membership unions are the Service Employees International Union with a membership over 500,000, of whom more than 200,000 are public employees; the International Brotherhood of Teamsters with approximately 80,000 public employee members; and the Amalgamated Transit Union with approximately 90,000 public employee members. Many other unions have mixed memberships. Interests in mixed membership unions are divided between public and private sector contingents, leading to some concern about how strongly they will represent public employee interests. However, they have the vast resources of the parent union behind them and are effective in marshaling support in the political process.

Public employee associations are the second type of representative in public sector collective bargaining. Some associations on the state and local levels have existed for many years. Although originally organized to improve employee opportunities and the status of public employees, the associations have redirected their activities toward collective bargaining.[13] Because of their original purposes, they tend to be less in favor of strikes and instead rely heavily on public relations and lobbying. They are becoming increasingly militant, however, as the competition for membership grows between them and the unions.

Professional associations, the third category, have also been organized for a long time to better the status of their professions and members. However, their membership is much more limited than that of public employee associations, in that educational or occupational criteria are imposed for membership. They have generally resisted joining the bargaining movement because they have viewed bargaining as unprofessional behavior. But the success of the unions and the employee associations in recruiting and gaining benefits for their members has stimulated professional groups to organize for collective bargaining.

Among the more active professional associations are the American Nurses Association (ANA), the National Association of Social Workers (NASW), and the American Association of University Professors (AAUP). The National Education Association (NEA) is the largest, with a membership of over 1.5 million, and is also one of the most active in the bargaining process. Its state affiliates decide on how deeply involved they wish to be in bargaining. The NEA and its affiliates provide some of the clearest evidence of the conflict in professional organizations over the collective bargaining issue. It has been pushed further into the bargaining process by the success of the American Federation of Teachers (AFT) in recruiting members and winning benefits for its members. To retain its membership, the NEA feels the necessity of bargaining. The AAUP has faced similar conflict as a representative of college and university faculty.

The variety of employee organizations in the bargaining process creates numerous approaches to issues in labor-management relations. Unions tend to be the most militant, although they vary greatly from one to another. Those unions associated with both private and public sector employees are usually more likely to support the right to strike, but police and fire fighter unions have certainly also done so in recent years. Employee and professional associations usually prefer public relations and lobbying to accomplish their objectives but have been pushed into more militant positions by the unions' success in their bargaining efforts. Similarly, some organizations, particularly employee associations, stress the independence of their affiliates, and the unions stress the resources their national organizations provide for them. All in all, approximately 50 percent of eligible public employees join unions or organizations that bargain for them, and almost 60 percent are actually represented in bargaining.

SCOPE OF BARGAINING

The labor relations policy also addresses the scope of bargaining or what can be bargained. The policy may make bargaining on issues either mandatory or permissive. Mandatory issues are those that must be bargained, and permissive issues are those that may be bargained if both parties wish to do so. There are also prohibited issues, that is, those that cannot be bargained according to the policy. In the national government, for example, wages and salaries cannot be bargained, and in many state and local governments, negotiators may be prohibited from bargaining on such items as assignment of personnel or decisions on the nature of the service to be delivered. Discriminatory provisions cannot be included in agreements in any jurisdiction.

A conflict arises over the scope of bargaining because management wishes to maintain as much management prerogative as possible in decisions, and labor wishes to share in that responsibility. That conflict usually leads to a definition of what items can and cannot be bargained. Generally, it is assumed that management rights exist independently of the collective bargaining relationship and until modified by that relationship. As with most other parts of labor relations policy, the scope of bargaining varies greatly by jurisdiction.[14]

Labor relations policy defines the basic rules under which labor relations takes place. The policy addresses issues other than those noted above, and they will be treated separately because of their particular significance in the bargaining process. Those issues include impasse resolution procedures, strikes, and contract administration. They will be examined after the next section, dealing with the negotiations themselves.

The Negotiating Process

Once it is determined what can be bargained and the employees have decided to use collective bargaining procedures and have selected a representative, the process may begin. Ordinarily, the employees will express their desire to bargain on an issue or issues by presenting proposals covering whatever items they wish to consider.[15] In recent years, it has been common for management also to draw up a list of demands to be considered at the negotiating table. Thus management now sees the process as a proactive rather than a reactive one. Once the proposals have been exchanged, the two sides meet to determine what procedures or ground rules will govern the negotiations. The proposals may be exchanged before the first meeting or at the meeting, depending on the particular case.

After each side makes and explains its proposals, each studies the other's positions so that reactions and counterproposals can be made.

These reactions and counterproposals become the focus of the negotiating process. Before the actual negotiations, however, each side has spent a lot of time in preparation. To be prepared, each side must be well versed in personnel rules and regulations and how they are implemented, as well as in the legal limitations imposed on personnel practices. Each side will also review the previous agreement and any problems that have occurred under it. Of particular interest will be any grievances filed under the current agreement. In addition, each party normally costs out its proposals and collects data on economic indicators, productivity, budget and revenue projections, and wages and salaries in similar and surrounding jurisdictions. Armed with these data, the negotiators are ready to begin negotiating over their proposals.

The behavior of the parties in the negotiations becomes extremely important, and posturing is common. One or the other party may decide to take an aggressive, challenging, hard-line approach on every item, hoping to wear down the other side. Or the strategy may be to focus on a few issues that are of particular importance and make concessions on other issues. Yet another approach is to appear conciliatory in order to establish goodwill. Often participants attempt to impress their own constituents as much as their adversaries in the negotiations. The strategy chosen normally depends on how far apart the parties and how important the issues are. Relative political power also becomes a factor in the public sector, as was illustrated by some of the examples cited earlier, particularly in New York City where employee organizations can bring other political forces into play. The Professional Air Traffic Controllers Organization (PATCO), however, miscalculated its power to influence management through appeals to citizens and the business community.

Most collective bargaining ends in agreement at the negotiating table. Then each side has to take the agreement back to its constituency for approval. The members of the employee organization vote on ratification of the agreement. If they vote no, more negotiation will be necessary. If yes, management then usually must go to the relevant legislative body for approval and funding. Occasionally a city council or school board rejects an agreement, in which case the negotiations must be restarted, but ordinarily the agreement wins approval. At the state and national levels, specific legislative approval is not usually required, but in states in which salary and fringe benefits are bargained, funding for the provisions does require legislative appropriations, and thus indirect approval.

Impasse Resolution Procedures

If the parties do not reach an agreement at the negotiating table, there are several alternatives available to attempt to resolve the impasse. These alternatives are called impasse procedures and include mediation, fact finding, arbitration, and referendum. All use outside parties.

MEDIATION

Mediation is used by most jurisdictions that permit bargaining. In mediation a neutral individual—usually trained in labor relations—tries to get the two parties to resolve their differences through compromise. Though they cannot impose decisions on the parties, the mediators meet with each party and discuss the points of disagreement and how they might be reconciled. Then they recommend solutions to the parties in hopes that the parties will work out the differences themselves.

FACT FINDING

Fact finding is a variation of the mediation process. In fact finding, a neutral third party works with both parties to the dispute and conducts a formal investigation of the issues separating them. The fact finder then issues a formal report stating the "facts" of the situation. The intent is that by formally pinpointing the differences, the report will bring pressure to bear on the parties to resolve their differences. In some instances, such as in New York and Wisconsin, the reports must be made public, in the hopes that public opinion and pressure will cause the parties to settle. Fact finding is usually employed if mediation fails, and the majority of states that allow bargaining also permit its use.

ARBITRATION

If fact finding fails, the next step is more controversial. Because public jurisdictions generally prohibit strikes, some form of final, binding decision becomes attractive. The alternative normally available is arbitration. In arbitration a neutral third party has the authority to impose a settlement or, in the case of advisory arbitration, is asked to recommend a solution. Conventional arbitration is binding in the sense that if parties go to arbitration, they are bound to accept the arbitrator's decision. The arbitrator does much the same work as a mediator or fact finder does: evaluates the situation and then decides on an equitable solution. The difference is that the decision is binding. In some instances, final-offer arbitration is used. Each party presents the arbitrator with its final offer for settlement, and the arbitrator then selects the better of the two. The logic behind this approach is that the parties can be expected to offer the most reasonable solution possibly out of fear that the arbitrator may choose a worse settlement proposed by the other party. Connecticut and Indiana use forms of final-offer arbitration.

Arbitration is also often differentiated as voluntary or compulsory. Voluntary arbitration means that the parties voluntarily choose to go to arbitration. In compulsory arbitration they have no choice but to go to arbitration at some specified point. Thus, the law may require arbitration if mediation has been attempted and failed or after a certain number of days of impasse. The difference between these two types of arbitration is only in how the parties arrive at arbitration: once the process starts, it is the same.

A combination form of impasse resolution is the med-arb approach, as used in Wisconsin. In med-arb, a mediator attempts to resolve the impasse. If unsuccessful, the mediator then becomes an arbitrator. This system is supposed to be more efficient in that the mediator already knows the situation and so, as an arbitrator, does not have to spend time becoming familiar with it. Knowing that the same person is going to arbitrate if mediation is unsuccessful may also encourage the two parties to work out their own differences along the lines of the mediator's suggestions.

REFERENDUM

The fourth impasse procedure is the voter referendum, in which either party may take the contested issues to the public. Colorado uses this method. The experience with this approach is not extensive enough to have provided much evidence concerning its effect. As with final-offer arbitration, the referendum approach can bring pressure to get the decision made through the negotiating process so as to avoid potentially harsher agreements from the outside.

The impasse procedures outlined here progress from the least to the most coercive in terms of outside parties' being able to impose settlements. However, there is interaction among the processes. The developments in mediation and fact finding provide part of the basis for the arbitration process if it progresses that far. Variations in each of the procedures may also combine elements from one or more of the "pure" impasse procedures noted.

Strikes

If these procedures are not available or do not resolve the impasse, employees may decide that they have no alternative but to strike. Although most jurisdictions prohibit strikes by public employees, there has been no dearth of strikes in the public sector (see Table 7-1). Since 1980, however, the number of public sector strikes has dropped. The PATCO experience, high unemployment, and the public's disaffection with labor unions all probably contributed to less militance by employee organizations. Opposition to strikes is evident to the extent that all but nine states prohibit strikes; and where they are permitted, they are generally limited in that only certain types of employees may engage in them. Police, fire, hospital, and correctional personnel are usually excluded.

States such as Vermont, Pennsylvania, and Hawaii give public employees limited rights to strike, but more common are strict prohibitions. Even where prohibited, however, strikes are numerous. The beginning of every school year is marked by teachers' strikes across the country. Chicago school teachers went to work without a contract in 1984, but with no progress in negotiations, they struck shortly before Christmas. Similarly, strikes of Denver transit workers in 1982 and police in Corona, California, in 1983 were illegal. But implementing legislation banning strikes is not always easy. Officials, including judges, are often reluctant to enforce no-strike legislation by jailing strikers because of the possible martyr effect. The people jailed become heroes to other employees, and the strikes are likely to grow, along with public sympathy for employees willing to go to such lengths for their cause.

As noted earlier, however, some jurisdictions have been very effective in handling strikes. The firing of the PATCO strikers broke the strike and has been used as a symbol of management's tougher stance. But even though successful in the short run, such tactics may damage the morale of other employees and the credibility of management with its work force. The long-term impact is not clear. When labor regains

Table 1. Work stoppages by level of government, 1942–80 (Workers and days idle in thousands)

Year	Total[1] Number of stoppages	Total[1] Workers involved	Total[1] Days idle during year	Federal Government Number of stoppages	Federal Government Workers involved	Federal Government Days idle during year	State Government Number of stoppages	State Government Workers involved	State Government Days idle during year	Local government[2] Number of stoppages	Local government[2] Workers involved	Local government[2] Days idle during year
1942	—	—	—							39	6.0	23.7
1943	—	—	—				2	0.4	8.0	51	10.2	48.5
1944	—	—	—							34	5.3	57.7
1945	—	—	—							32	3.4	20.0
1946	—	—	—			1				61	9.6	51.0
1947	—	—	—							14	1.1	7.3
1948	—	—	—							25	1.4	8.8
1949	—	—	—							7	2.9	10.3
1950	—	—	—							26	4.0	32.7
1951	—	—	—							36	4.9	28.8
1952	—	—	—							49	8.1	33.4
1953	—	—	—							30	6.3	53.4
1954	—	—	—							9	1.8	9.6
1955	—	—	—						(3)	16	1.3	6.7
1956	—	—	—							27	3.5	11.1
1957	—	—	—							12	.8	4.4
1958	15	1.7	7.5				1	(3)	.8	14	1.7	7.4
1959	25	2.0	10.5				1	.2	.5	21	1.6	8.8
1960	36	28.6	58.4	—	—	—	4	(3)	(3)	33	27.6	57.2
1961	28	6.6	15.3	—	—	—	3	.4	1.6	28	6.6	15.3
1962	28	31.1	79.1	5	4.2	33.8	2	1.0	1.2	21	25.3	43.1
1963	29	4.8	15.4	—	—	—	2	1.7	2.3	27	4.6	13.3
1964	41	22.7	70.8	—	—	—	4	.3	2.2	37	22.5	67.7
1965	42	11.9	146.0	—	—	—	—	.3	3.2[4]	42	11.9	145.0
1966	142	105.0	455.0	—	—	—	9	3.1	1.3	133	102.0	449.0
1967	181	132.0	1,250.0	—	—	—	12	4.7	16.3	169	127.0	1,230.0
1968	254	201.8	2,545.2	3	1.7	9.6	16	9.3	42.8	235	190.9	2,492.8
1969	411	160.0	745.7	2	.6	1.1	37	20.5	152.4	372	139.0	592.2
1970	412	333.5	2,023.2	3	155.8	648.3	23	8.8	44.6	386	168.9	1,330.5
1971	329	152.6	901.4	2	1.0	8.1	23	14.5	81.8	304	137.1	811.6
1972	375	142.1	1,257.3	—	—	—	40	27.4	273.7	335	114.7	983.5
1973	387	196.4	2,303.9	1	.5	4.6	29	12.3	133.0	357	183.7	2,166.3
1974	384	160.7	1,404.2	2	.5	1.4	34	24.7	86.4	348	135.4	1,316.3
1975	478	318.5	2,204.4	1	(3)	(3)	32	66.6	300.5	446	252.0	1,903.9
1976	378	180.7	1,690.7	2	.4	.5	25	33.8	148.2	352	146.3	1,542.6
1977	413	170.2	1,765.7	—	—	—	44	33.7	181.9	367	136.2	1,583.3
1978	481	193.7	1,706.7	1	4.8	27.8	45	17.9	180.2	435	171.0	1,498.8
1979	593	254.1	2,982.5	—	—	—	57	48.6	515.5	536	205.5	2,467.1
1980	536	223.6	2,347.8	1	.9	7.2	45	10.0	99.7	493	212.7	2,240.9

The Bureau of Labor Statistics has published data on stoppages in government in its annual reports since 1942. Before that year, they had been included in a miscellaneous category—other nonmanufacturing industries. From 1942 through 1957, data refer only to stoppages in administrative, protective, and sanitary services of government. Stoppages in establishments owned by governments were classified in their appropriate industry; for example, public schools and libraries were included in education services, not in government. Beginning in 1958, stoppages in such establishments were included under the government classification. Stoppages in publicly owned utilities, transportation, and schools were reclassified back to 1947, but a complete reclassification was not attempted. After 1957, dashes indicate that no data were reported.

[2] Includes all stoppages at the county, city, and special district level.
[3] Fewer than 100.
[4] Idleness in 1965 resulted from 2 stoppages that began in 1964.
NOTE: Because of rounding, sums of individual items may not equal totals.

its political clout, as is surely to happen, management is likely to face militant employee organizations.

Contract Administration

Once an agreement is reached, it must be implemented; the process for doing so is by contract administration. This process gives meaning to the agreement and is thus an important part of collective bargaining. Implementation is generally management's responsibility, but the employees will react to what they perceive to be management's misinterpretations of the agreement. Many provisions in a contract may be vague, causing problems in interpretation, or parties may disagree on what is meant by such terms as *reasonable time, just cause,* or *normal practices.* Similarly, unanticipated situations may develop and must be dealt with under the contract's terms.

Although the labor relations office may have overall responsibility for implementing the agreement, the first line supervisor is the key person in contract administration. He or she has continuous contact with the employees and thus effectively carries out the agreement's provisions. To make sure that the supervisors understand the contract and will implement it consistently, they are usually given training on the contract. The contract's provisions are interpreted for the supervisors, who are also carefully instructed about all the contents of the contract.

Employees may complain about the way a part of the agreement is or is not implemented, and normally one individual is chosen as the shop steward. This steward represents the employees and tries to resolve their complaints. The steward also monitors the contract's implementation to ensure its compliance with the agreement and raises objections as appropriate. Most of management's contact with the employees concerning the contract's administration is through the steward.

Despite efforts to implement the agreement correctly, problems often develop, and the parties may not be able to resolve disagreements over specific provisions. In most bargaining agreements, this eventuality is provided for by grievance arbitration. The process normally calls for the employee with a complaint to file a written grievance with his or her immediate supervisor. The complaint may be settled at this level, but usually the issue can be appealed for resolution up through top management. If the parties are still unable to resolve the issue, arbitration will be invoked. The process is essentially the same as in the arbitration procedure for resolving negotiation impasses. If there is no grievance arbitration clause in the collective bargaining agreement, personnel or civil service rules will provide for dealing with complaints over the agreement's implementation.

Impact of Public Sector Bargaining

The effects of collective bargaining are felt in all areas of management and service delivery. There are clear implications for financial management, budgeting, personnel and planning, and the roles of employees and managers in the system.

In the area of financial management and budgeting, collective bargaining agreements often lock the jurisdiction into positions from which it cannot easily extricate itself. As the effects of taxpayer's demands clearly illustrate, voters believe that collective bargaining adds to the cost of government. The empirical evidence continues to be rather confusing, however. Recent studies suggest that the impact has been to increase the cost of government but that the overall increases have been relatively small.[16] Because personnel costs typically make up 70 to 90 percent of a jurisdiction's budget, it is inevitable that increased personnel costs will affect the cost of government unless there is a reduction in personnel and services. As a result, jurisdictions try to offset personnel costs by increasing productivity. Clearly, the bargaining process puts costs under constant scrutiny, thus providing the potential for containment and the elimination of unnecessary items.

Budgeting processes are also affected by bargaining. Negotiation and agreement typically take place before the budget is drawn up; thus, flexibility in budgeting may be diminished. If management or the legislative body refuses to appropriate funds to cover the agreement's costs, including salaries and wages, problems with the employee organization are certain to arise. Though legislative bodies have the power to adopt governmental budgets, the bargaining process actually reduces that authority and effectively places it in the hands of the bargaining parties. Budgeting and planning thus become difficult when the decision makers' flexibility is hampered.

The personnel function is greatly affected by the bargaining process because it is difficult to limit the scope of bargaining. Because of the many states that permit bargaining on all aspects of the employment situation, all elements of the personnel system can be bargained. It seems clear that merit system principles and personnel rules and regulations will increasingly become the subject of negotiation and will change in the process.[17]

For management the effects of collective bargaining are many. Traditionally, management has taken the position that bargaining is detrimental to its ability to manage. There is no question that with collective bargaining, management must share its power to govern and thus will have much less discretion. However, management can and does reap benefits from the bargaining process if it is willing to do so. Lanning S. Mosher pointed out that management can be improved through the bargaining process because the bargaining focuses attention on it as a team. By identifying management's weakness and negotiating training needs, the bargaining process provides leverage for obtaining the resources necessary to prepare for negotiating and working with labor organizations.[18] Management is also under pressure to do a good job when it knows its activities will be under scrutiny in the bargaining process.

Collective bargaining has the potential of creating a wide variety of types of working conditions as each group of employees bargains with management. But with a standard general policy under which agreements are bargained, the process can produce decisions that reflect a general perspective rather than the particular concerns of the moment or situation. In other words, it helps establish a general policy within which decisions can be made.

For employees, bargaining also has many effects, not the least of which is the ability to help decide what the working conditions are to be. Workers often find that unionization and bargaining help them develop a consciousness; this has been particularly true of employees in jobs such as sanitation and garbage collection. During the 1960s, racial minorities who were relegated to these positions found unionization to be both a way of gaining dignity as human beings and a force for racial and social justice. Generally, employees consider that collective bargaining protects them against arbitrariness in personnel and managerial decisions. Also, because employees participate in the decision-making processes, they are likely to be more committed to the organization than when management unilaterally dictates policy. In fact, management often has an ally in the employee representative in getting its policies across. Employees are much more receptive to decisions that are explained by one of their own; otherwise they may be obstacles to change and accommodation to management's desires.[19]

Summary

Public sector collective bargaining was one of the most visible elements of public personnel management in the 1960s and 1970s. During the 1980s the growth in the movement leveled off considerably as the political and economic environments became less supportive. Facing financial and political constraints, public employee unions were forced to reconsider their strategies. They therefore have become less militant and seem more conciliatory to management. Management in the public sector, however, seems more strident, as it sees the opportunity to use its new clout to retrieve some of the issues it gave up in earlier days.

Despite the reduced popularity of collective bargaining and unions, public managers still must deal with the process. Thus, public policy provides for a variety of ways of recognizing unions and bargaining with them. There are also many alternatives for dealing with impasses. Although illegal in most places, public employees do strike frequently.

Clearly, management will have to continue to bargain with employees, but the nature of the bargaining relationship is always evolving. New issues arise that provide the basis for continued efforts by unions. Currently, comparable worth is an issue that has been embraced by public employee labor unions and helps sustain their momentum.

NOTES

1. See Thomas R. Brooks, *Toil and Trouble*, 2nd ed. (New York: Dell Pub. Co., Inc., 1971); and Philip L. Martin, *Contemporary Labor Relations* (Belmont, Calif.: Wadsworth, 1979), for excellent histories of the labor movement, and especially Chapters 23 and 8, respectively, for reviews of the public sector.

2. See Sara Silbiger, "The Missing Public: Collective Bargaining Employment," *Public Personnel Management*, 4 (September-October 1975), 290–299; and Clyde W. Summers, "Public Bargaining: A Political Perspective," *Yale Law Journal*, 83 (May 1974), 1156–2000, at pp. 1160–1164.

3. James W. Singer, "The Limited Power of Federal Worker Unions," *National Journal*, September 22, 1978, pp. 1547–1551.

4. Summers, pp. 1166–1168.

5. See *Summary of Public Sector Labor Relations Policies* (Washington, D.C.: U.S. Department of Labor, Labor-Management Services Administration, 1981).

6. The sovereignty issue is discussed fully by Louis V. Immundo, Jr., "Federal Government Sovereignty and Its Effect on Labor-Management Relations," *Labor Law Journal*, (March 1975), 146–151; and delegation is examined by Robert S. Lorch, *Democratic Process and Administrative Law* (Detroit: Wayne State University Press, 1969).

7. For analyses of the privilege doctrine, see Philip L. Martin, "Return to the Privilege Right Doctrine in Public Employment," *Labor Law Journal*, (June 1977), 361–368; David H. Rosenbloom, "Public Personnel Administration and the Constitution: An Emergent Approach," *Public Administration Review*, 35 (January-February 1975), 52–59; and David H. Rosenbloom, "The Source of Continuing Conflict Between the Constitution and Public Personnel Management," *Review of Public Personnel Administration*, 2 (Fall 1981), 2–18.

8. This discussion is based on the conflicting ideas of Clyde W. Summers, "Public-Sector Bargaining: Problems of Governmental Decision Making," *Cincinnati Law Review*, 44 (1975), 668–679; and R. Theodore Clark, Jr., "Politics and Public Employee Unionism: Some Recommendations for an Emerging Problem," *Cincinnati Law Review*, 44 (1975), 680–689.

9. Clark, "Politics and Public Employee Unionism," p. 684.

10. For example, Silbiger, "The Missing Public"; George Bennett, "The Elusive Public Interest in Labor Disputes," *Labor Law Journal*, 25 (November 1974), 678–681; and Raymond D. Horton, *Municipal Labor Relations in New York City* (New York: Praeger, 1973).

11. Summers, "Public-Sector Bargaining," pp. 674–677.

12. Ibid., p. 670.

13. See James F. Marshall, "Public Employee Associations: Roles and Programs," *Public Personnel Management*, 3 (September-October 1974), 415–424, for a review of such organizations.

14. A good review of state, local, and national policies on this and other issues can be found in *Summary of Public Sector Labor Relations Policies*.

15. A step-by-step outline of the process is provided by Florida Department of Community Affairs, *Collective Bargaining*, rev. ed. (Tallahassee: State of Florida Department of Community Affairs, November 1977). This publication is part of an excellent series published by the department with IPA support.

16. For two good reviews, see Ralph Jones, *Public-Sector Labor Relations: An Evaluation of Policy-related Research* (Cambridge, Mass.: Ballinger, 1977), and Richard C. Kearney, *Labor Relations in the Public Sector* (New York: Marcel Dekker, 1984), chaps. 4 and 5.

17. These issues are discussed in detail in Muriel M. Morse, "The Impact of Collective Bargaining on the Merit System," *Public Service*, 5 (June 1978), 1–4.

18. Lanning S. Mosher, "Facing the Realities of Public Employee Bargaining," *Public Personnel Management*, 7 (July-August 1978), 243–248.

19. For an example of a case in which management's directives were not accepted, see Wes Uhlman, "Standing Up to Union Pressures," *Nation's Cities*, 13 (November 1975), 12–14.

SUGGESTED READINGS

Alward, James M. "Toward Negotiations." *Public Personnel Management*, 13 (Summer 1984), 191–196.

Campbell, Edwin S., Jr. "Strategies for a New Ball Game: Agency Personnel Regulations and Collective Bargaining." *Public Personnel Management*, 13 (Summer 1984), 185–189.

Cayer, N. Joseph, and Sherry S. Dickerson. *Labor Management Relations in the Public Sector: An Annotated Bibliography*. New York: Garland Publishing, 1984.

Clark, R. Theodore, Jr. "Politics and Public Employee Unionism: Some Recommendations for an Emerging Problem." *Cincinnati Law Review*, 44 (1975), 680–689.

Ermer-Bott, Virginia, and Alan Saltzstein. "The Impact of Proposition 13 on Labor-Management Relations in California." *Public Personnel Management*, 10 (Summer 1981), 203–206.

Feigenbaum, Charles. "Final Arbitration: Better Theory Than Practice." *Industrial Relations*, 14 (October 1975), 311–317.

Fortier, Richard G. "An AFGE Local: An Examination of Factors Contributing to Union Strength in the Public Sector." *Public Personnel Management*, 13 (Fall 1984), 265–292.

Graham, Harry. "Arbitration Results in the Public Sector." *Public Personnel Management*, 11 (Summer 1982), 112–117.

Horton, Raymond D. *Municipal Labor Relations in New York City: Lessons of the Lindsay–Wagner Years*. New York: Praeger, 1973.

Jones, Ralph. *Public-Sector Labor Relations: An Evaluation of Policy-related Research*. Cambridge, Mass.: Ballinger 1977.

Kearney, Richard C. *Labor Relations in the Public Sector*. New York: Marcel Dekker, 1984.

McCabe, Douglas M. "Labor Relations, Collective Bargaining, and Performance Appraisal in the Federal Government Under the Civil Service Reform Act of 1978." *Public Personnel Management*, 13 (Summer 1984), 133–146.

Nash, Michael D., and Nolan J. Argyle. "Old Mother Hubbard Revisited: Comments on the Reliability of the Collective Bargaining Literature." *Review of Public Personnel Administration*, 4 (Spring 1984), 1–12.

Stieber, Jack. *Public Employee Unionism: Structure, Growth, and Policy*. Washington, D.C.: Brookings Institution, 1973.

Sulzner, George T. "Politics, Labor Relations, and Public Personnel Management: Retrospect and Prospect." *Policy Studies Journal*, 11 (December 1982), 279–289.

Summers, Clyde W. "Public Bargaining: A Political Perspective." *Yale Law Journal*, 83 (May 1974), 1156–2000.
————. "Public-Sector Bargaining: Problems of Governmental Decision Making." *Cincinnati Law Review*, 44 (1975), 668–679.
Veglahn, Peter A. "Public Sector Strike Penalties and Their Appeal." *Public Personnel Management*, 12 (Summer 1983), 196–205.
Wellington, Harry H., and Ralph K. Winter, Jr. *The Unions and the Cities.* Washington, D.C.: Brookings Institution, 1971.

Case 7.1: The Librarians

When collective bargaining came to the state university, the faculty and professional staff were organized as one unit for bargaining purposes. In the first few years, developing methods of articulating employee concerns and catching up in salary with comparable universities were the paramount concerns for all members. Now that salaries are reasonable and lines of communication with the administration have been formalized, differences within the bargaining unit are beginning to surface.

In particular, the librarians feel that their interests are not well represented. In a bargaining unit that represents two thousand people, they number three hundred. The faculty dominate the organization and seem uninterested in the special concerns of the library personnel. The librarians thus have petitioned the Public Employee Relations Board to establish a bargaining unit of their own.

INSTRUCTIONS:

You are the hearing officer for the Public Employee Relations Board.

1. What information will you want to consider in making your recommendation?
2. Considering the information you are likely to receive, what recommendation will you make?
3. Justify your recommendation.

Case 7.2: Was It a Strike?

The city police force went on strike, even though state law prohibits public employees from striking. They went on strike because they were unable to get any relief from the long hours of overtime they had worked since the recent budget cuts.

Sonja Ki stayed home from her job as patrol officer during the strike. Because the strike was illegal, the union was decertified, and all those participating were fired. Ki appealed her firing to the City Employee Relations Board.

INSTRUCTIONS:

You are the hearing officer assigned to Ki's appeal.

1. What information do you need?
2. What are you likely to recommend?
3. What is your justification?

Some information you should consider:
Ki did not appear for work during the four days of the strike.
She did not call in to explain her absence.
She has an excellent record of service during her three years on the police force.

8

Public Personnel and Democracy

The relationship of public personnel management to democracy is a continuing issue in our political system. Because the public service is supposed to be responsible and accountable to the general public in a democratic polity, public personnel administration is continually examined in terms of how accountable and responsive the public service is. This chapter will focus on how the personnel system and its employees foster accountability and responsibility. Democracy in personnel systems pertains to (1) the bureaucracy's representativeness, (2) equity in dealing with employees and clientele, and (3) advocacy administration and citizen participation.

Representative Bureaucracy

Representative bureaucracy is a concept that has been important to public personnel management from the very beginning of our government. As noted earlier, President Washington and his successors were concerned with representing influential political groups in their administrations, and the Jeffersonians and Jacksonians made clear that government offices should be held by people supportive of them. Political leaders at all levels have been sensitive to using appointments to public office as a means of rewarding supporters or consolidating the support of others. Thus, a form of representativeness has always been a major part of personnel decisions. In recent years, the concept has been refined and now includes a concern for the representation of all elements of society, regardless of whether or not they have political power. But of course, if they have political clout, their concerns are likely to be considered more quickly.

One concern with representative bureaucracy pertains to active and passive representation, as suggested by Mosher.[1]

In active representation, a representative is expected to act in the interest of sectors of society, regardless of what group the representative belongs to. In passive representation, one is assumed to represent the interests of the group from which one comes. Thus in passive representation the representatives' personal characteristics and social background are important, and advocates of such representation believe the bureaucracy should be a mirror image of the society as a whole. Passive representation is exemplified by goals and timetables that affirmative action plans use to make the public service accurately reflect the population.

There are grave differences, though, in the ways that people perceive the linkage between active and passive representation. The assumption underlying equal employment opportunity and affirmative action programs is that passive representation will eventually lead to the active representation of those groups who are becoming members of the bureaucracy. That assumption is the subject of much study and disagreement.[2] Despite these differences of opinion, government acts on the premise that all the various groups in our society should be represented and will influence the public service in its actions. Another important consideration is that minority groups are more likely to feel comfortable in dealing with bureaucrats from their own groups. Affirmative action has as one of its intended effects making bureaucracies and their programs more accessible to groups previously denied such access. Thus, as Rosenbloom and Kinnard observed, representative bureaucracy is advocated for two reasons: (1) to provide distributive justice and equal opportunity and (2) to allow for input from all social and economic groups.[3]

DEVELOPMENT OF AN UNREPRESENTATIVE BUREAUCRACY

Although the Jeffersonians and Jacksonians "democratized" the public service in many ways, the United States public service has never really been representative of the society as a whole. Among the many reasons for this are political considerations and traditions. Some also argue that the bureaucracy, by its nature, requires skills that are not distributed throughout the population.[4] As a result, bureaucracies often discriminate in favor of middle-class people because they have the necessary skills. The reasons that many people do not acquire such skills are often political and social, and they will be the focus of this analysis. Jacksonian Democracy opened the public service to the common man, but the new participants were still only white males. The reign of the spoils system entrenched the white male in the public service because friends and relatives of those already holding political power reaped the rewards. By the time minorities and women achieved some political influence, the spoils system had been fairly well destroyed as a means of staffing the federal bureaucracy and was on the way out in many state and local jurisdictions as well. With the blanketing-in procedures used for extending civil service protection, the white male was more or less assured of control over the bureaucracy and the selection of new members. Consequently, the newly emerging groups had few opportunities to enter the system.

Although the Civil War emancipated the slaves, the political power of the black population was minimal until after the middle of the twentieth century. A gradual process of judicial and legislative extension of rights to minorities and women took place during the late nineteenth and early twentieth centuries. The Nineteenth Amendment to the Constitution was supposed to open the doors to women, but they, like blacks, found that constitutionally guaranteed rights do not automatically translate into rights in practice. Instead, much effort is required to realize those rights.[5]

The mid-twentieth century witnessed a concern for the rights of minorities and individuals alike. The Warren Court and its libertarian and civil rights orientation jolted the consciences of citizens and political leaders, resulting in many court decisions and much legislation prohibiting discrimination against minorities, and eventually women. In employment practices, it became illegal to discriminate on the basis of race, religion, sex, and so on. Although these nondiscrimination policies helped, they fell far short of actually providing equality of opportunity, particularly in high-level positions.

FROM NONDISCRIMINATION TO AFFIRMATIVE ACTION

Because nondiscrimination laws and regulations failed to achieve the expected results, government leaders instituted new approaches. President Kennedy, the recipient of strong minority group support, emphasized positive action to promote the well-being of those who had previously been discriminated against. Blacks, in particular, were brought into prominent positions in the public service. President Lyndon Johnson, eager to shed his Texas and southern identification for a national constituency, increased the pressure to employ blacks. Minority group support was a concern of President Nixon as well, who took a special interest in Hispanics, as did President Reagan in his 1984 reelection campaign. As women developed greater political consciousness in the late 1960s and 1970s, the leaders of both parties and at all levels of government began to demonstrate concern for women's rights (and votes) by making efforts to increase the public employment of women. In the 1984 presidential election, the gender gap became a major issue, as the Democratic party nominated a female vice-presidential candidate to attempt to exploit their perception of the Reagan administration's lack of concern for women's issues. The Reagan administration explained that they did not talk of women's issues, they just employed women in prominent positions. But one of the complaints of minorities and women is that the Reagan administration does not emphasize equal employment and affirmative action issues and has, in fact, made efforts to weaken agencies such as the Civil Rights Commission and the Equal Employment Opportunity Commission.

Equal employment opportunity and affirmative action are the two main approaches to expanding employment opportunities for women and minorities. Equal employment opportunity does not necessarily result in greater employment; rather, it merely requires that all groups have the same chance to compete for positions and are treated equally once employed. Of particular concern is that personnel decisions be made on the basis of criteria that are pertinent to the work. Equal opportunity requires neutrality on issues other than merit or ability in the personnel process. The Civil Rights Act of 1964 provides the basic requirements for equality of opportunity. Because that act applies to private sector employers only, the 1972 Equal Employment Opportunity Act was passed to extend the policy to state and local governments.

Although guarantees of equal employment opportunity are important, they do not take effect on their own. Enforcement agencies and monitoring mechanisms have therefore been created to see that the acts are implemented. The Equal Employment Opportunity Commission and the Civil Rights Commission are the principal agencies at the national level that have enforcement responsibilities. Each department or agency that distributes grants or services or has contracts with other employers, including state and local governments, has some type of compliance office to make sure that equal employment opportunity exists. Revenue-sharing funds now also come with the provision that they can be suspended if a court or administrative agency finds discrimination in the recipient jurisdiction's services or employment. Monitoring agencies have difficulty in gaining compliance because they are usually inadequately staffed and often are on the functional agencies' periphery. Standards of what constitutes equal opportunity also tend to be vague and hard to enforce. As a result of these problems, the concept of affirmative action developed.

Affirmative action requires employers to make a conscious effort to eliminate from their personnel systems intended and unintended discrimination as well as the effects of past discrimination. Thus it calls for an examination of all personnel functions to identify possible barriers to equal employment opportunity so that they can be removed. The key to determining whether discrimination exists is to be found not in the policy's intent but, rather, in what occurs as a result of that policy.

Affirmative action plans are not uniformly mandatory. However, granting agencies may require them, or compliance agencies and courts may require plans from those jurisdictions in which a complaint of discrimination has been found to be valid. And many jurisdictions develop plans voluntarily.

Developing an affirmative action plan requires analyzing all personnel policies and procedures to determine whether they contain any potentially discriminatory features. Any features that have a differential impact on women or minorities are suspect and should be carefully evaluated and changed if they cannot be justified as job relevant. The focal point of much affirmative action is in the recruitment and selection phases of personnel actions, although all aspects of the process are important (see Table 8-1).

Although affirmative action theoretically calls for the use of strict merit procedures, by requiring that only job-relevant factors be considered, critics have complained that in practice, affirmative action results in reverse discrimination. In other words, minorities and females are being given advantages to the detriment of white males.[6] The charge usually arises because of the use of goals for achieving balance in employment. Goals are established for the hiring, promotion, and so forth of females and minorities to bring them into the employment structure on a basis representative of their presence in the labor pool.

Table 8-1 Establishing an Affirmative Action Plan

The most important measure of an affirmative action program is its results. Extensive efforts to develop procedures, analyses, data collection systems, report forms, and policy statements are meaningless unless the end product can measure yearly improvement in hiring, training, and promoting minorities and females in all parts of the organization. The only realistic basis for evaluating a program to increase opportunity for minorities and females is its actual impact on these persons.

The essence of an affirmative action program should be
• Establish strong agency policy and commitment.
• Assign responsibility and authority for the program to a top agency official.
• Analyze the present work force to identify jobs, departments, and units in which minorities and females are underutilized.
• Set specific, measurable, and attainable hiring and promotion goals, with target dates, in each area of underutilization.
• Make every manager and supervisor responsible and accountable for helping meet these goals.
• Reevaluate job descriptions and hiring criteria to ensure that they reflect actual job needs.
• Find minorities and females who qualify or can become qualified to fill goals.
• Review and revise all employment procedures to ensure that they do not have discriminatory effects and that they help attain goals.
• Focus on getting minorities and females into upward mobility and relevant training pipelines to which they have not had previous access.
• Develop systems to monitor and measure progress regularly. If results are not satisfactory to meet goals, find out why, and make the necessary changes.

Source: Adapted from U.S. Equal Employment Opportunity Commission, *Affirmative Action and Equal Employment: A Guidebook for Employers* (Washington, D.C.: U.S. Government Printing Office, 1974), vol. 1, p. 3.

In the view of many, goals are nothing more than quotas that employers must meet so as to avoid being branded as discriminatory.

Enforcement or compliance agencies avoid using the term *quotas* and argue that their goals are different. Theoretically, these goals are targets that the employer attempts to attain. But circumstances may mean that those goals cannot be reached, and if they cannot, the employer normally has to explain why. Therefore, many employers feel constrained to achieve them, regardless of how they do so. They then often feel justified in hiring less-qualified minorities and females to meet their goals. In most cases, however, affirmative action does not require such reverse discrimination. Compliance agencies are frequently at fault for their single-minded concern with meeting goals, but most such agencies do recognize that circumstances do not always permit employers to meet all their anticipated goals and so make their judgments on the basis of good-faith efforts. Because employers sometimes feel pressured to discriminate in favor of minorities and women, critics of affirmative action argue that merit and competence are sacrificed to meet goals and timetables. Most critics believe that the quality of public service suffers from affirmative action efforts and accordingly base their opposition on that belief. Certainly there are also critics who have a self-interest in maintaining the status quo. Many employees and employee groups have been in the forefront of battles to protect their turf from intrusion by minorities and women. But as employee associations and unions have seen their memberships level off or decline, their stances have changed, and now they are often among the strongest advocates of minority and female causes.

The record so far does not indicate that the critics' fears are well founded. Although minorities and women are increasingly evident in government employment, they are not represented at all levels of employment in proportion to their percentage in the general population. The higher levels of management are still essentially the preserve of white males, although changes are being made.[7] Because of the disproportionate representation of females and minorities at the lower levels of public bureaucracies, there is now more attention on upward mobility programs and possible discrimination in promotion policies.

The ultimate goal of affirmative action is to make sure that factors irrelevant to the performance of duties are not considered in the employment process. In the short run, however, it may be necessary to consider sex and race in order to equalize the balance and redress past discrimination. Obviously the problem of discrimination goes far beyond employment practices and can be resolved only by seeing that all people have the opportunity to develop their abilities and talents through education and training. Until society achieves that goal, there will be a need for such policies as affirmative action.

Comparable Worth

Equal employment opportunity and affirmative action help open doors to all segments of society. With the present emphasis on eliminating discriminatory practices from public employment, new concerns have arisen. For example, females and minorities are often concentrated in certain types of jobs or occupations. In addition, the pay for the positions in which females and minorities are concentrated usually is significantly lower than for those jobs traditionally dominated by white males. These facts have led many advocates of equal opportunity to turn their attention to the issue of comparable worth. Comparable worth refers to equal pay for work of comparable value. The definition of comparable work is the source of much disagreement, as is the whole question of whether efforts should be made to institute comparable worth as a policy in public employment. Although most people agree with the general principle, many argue that it is inconsistent with our economic system and would wreak havoc with the economy. The Reagan administration seems to be on the side of the critics, as such Reagan appointees as the chairperson of the Civil Rights Commission and the staff director of that agency have been outspoken opponents of instituting comparable worth in the federal service. They also strongly urge the rest of the employment world not to adopt it.

The comparable worth issue arises from the fact that women consistently earn less than men. Overall, women earn approximately fifty-nine cents for every dollar that men earn. In the private sector, they earn only fifty-six cents per dollar of earnings by men and in the federal government approximately sixty-three cents. State and local governments have the best ratio, but women still earn only seventy-one cents per dollar earned by men.[8] Because women are concentrated in certain occupations and those occupations generally pay less than does the work dominated by males, they continually earn less than men. Even though the various nondiscrimination laws and the Equal Pay Act of 1963 had equity as a goal, they have not resolved this problem. The Equal Pay Act has usually been interpreted to mean that people doing the same work should be paid equally. The comparable worth concept raises the issue that different kinds of work can be comparable in the education, training, skills, knowledge and responsibility, and so on required to perform the job. Thus, nurses perform work that is comparable, according to those standards, to many male-dominated jobs but receive less pay because the work is dominated by women.

In order to determine the worth of a job, job evaluation is needed. The evaluation process is similar to that discussed in connection with position classification and is identifying each component of the job and then attaching a value to it. By summing the values of the components, the jobs' overall value can be determined. An organization's jobs are then placed in a hierarchy according to their values. This hierarchy is then compared with the pay accorded to positions by the organization's compensation plan.

The comparable worth issue has been highly visible since the late 1970s in the United States but actually had its origins in peace treaty negotiations after World War I.[9] The issue has come to the forefront through litigation, collective bargaining, and pressure by women's organizations. Some jurisdictions have also entered into the study of comparable worth because of concern for social justice. In 1981, the United States Supreme Court ruled in *County of Washington (Oregon) v Gunther*[10] that women could sue for discrimination in pay even if they were not doing exactly the same work as men were. Although the decision was not based on comparable worth as such, it did open the door for further litigation by the Court's abandoning a very narrow interpretation of Title VII of the Civil Rights Act of 1964. Since that time much litigation has been instituted across the country on behalf of women who feel they are being paid less than they should be for the jobs they are doing. Before 1981 they were not successful in such litigation, and the record is still spotty. After the *Gunther* decision, AFSCME sued the state of Washington, which had conducted a job evaluation of its work force beginning in 1973. Though the study and subsequent updates demonstrated inequitable pay, the state did not move to remedy the situation. Therefore, in 1981 AFSCME sued, and in 1983 a federal court ordered the state to compensate its underpaid employees. That case has stimulated more action on comparable worth across the country.

In addition to litigation, some jurisdictions have been struck over comparable worth. San Jose, California, was the site of such a strike in 1981. Eventually, the city council settled with the union, instituting comparable worth as a part of the city's personnel policy. In 1984, employees of Yale University were engaged in a bitter strike to open the door to comparable worth in a private organization. AFSCME and other unions have been very active in supporting comparable worth, in part as a way of increasing its female membership. The AFL-CIO also passed a resolution endorsing comparable worth in 1981 with a detailed policy statement on the issue.

Many jurisdictions have taken a less visible path to dealing with the issue. Colorado Springs, Colorado, for example, began working on comparable worth during the late 1970s. A cooperative effort of the personnel department, city management, and employees led to a job evaluation study and implementation of a comparable worth policy by the city. Many states and local governments have also been studying the issue, and some, such as Minnesota, have adopted comparable worth as policy for their jurisdictions. Canada also uses comparable worth for federal employees and contractors with the federal government. The concerns of critics that jurisdictions will be bankrupted by comparable worth do not seem to be apparent in those places that have adopted the policy.

Comparable worth is likely to remain an issue for some time. Because public officials fear the policy's financial consequences, they have strong arguments for resisting it. With leaders of agencies such as the Equal Employment Opportunity Commission and the Civil Rights Commission, as well as the Justice Department, testifying against the concept in Congress and elsewhere, its opponents have strong allies. Advocates of comparable worth, however, also have strong allies, in that courts seem increasingly sympathetic, and women's groups have been gaining much more political power in recent years. Finally, labor unions are likely to keep up the pressure in the collective bargaining process.

Equity

Advocates of the "New Public Administration" brought social equity to the attention of public administration study.[11] However, there is still much disagreement about what social equity means and who has responsibility for fostering it.[12] In public administration, social equity usually refers to the belief that administrators have the responsibility to mitigate the unequal distribution of benefits that results from our pluralistic political system. According to this view, many people are denied access, opportunity, and services because they do not have the political power that permits them to compete for the system's resources and benefits. Furthermore, it is the administrators' responsibility to redress the inequitable treatment meted out to minorities and the poor. But the problem for public administrators is that there are many publics to be served, and one group is not willing to permit its claims to be slighted in order to offer equitable services to another. The reductions in federal government programs as a result of the Reagan administration's "new federalism" have accentuated the concern over the issue of equitable service delivery among students of public policy. There is not much evidence to suggest that public administrators have embraced the New Public Administration's attachment to the social equity issue. At least there is no formal espousal of the view. But agencies at all levels of government do have more and more responsibility to respond to the needs of the minorities and the poor. Through affirmative action and citizen participation programs, agencies have been sensitized to the needs of these groups.

Advocacy and Participatory Administration

Some students of public administration feel that the only way to make the public service democratic is to democratize the decision-making processes within agencies and particularly to offer methods by which clientele and public interest groups can participate in administration.[13] Many programs of the Office of Economic Opportunity during the 1960s required citizen participation, and there have been carry-overs to programs at all levels of government. Even when not required, citizen and public interest groups have become increasingly involved in pressing their interests.

Citizen participation affects job design and the response of public employees to community needs. Often citizen participation means that employees are selected from the community served. Also, members of the community may be placed on advisory and monitoring boards. But because people from the community often lack the appropriate skills, jobs may have to be redesigned or training programs developed. On the other hand, people from the community usually understand the community and are loyal to it, thus tempering their loyalty to the agency or supervisor.

The purposes of citizen participation are generally to make administration more responsive to the public and to enhance the legitimacy of government programs and agencies. As Stephen Cupps found, citizen participation has been responsible for opening to public debate many issues that would otherwise have not had any public input.[14] Citizen and public interest groups have also caused issues to be raised and considered by governments that would have been content to ignore them. Because of their participation, such groups have been effective checks on governments and have stimulated greater public involvement in decision making.

Though the benefits of citizen participation are many, there are also numerous difficulties. As Cupps noted, citizen participation often encounters problems associated with (1) shortsightedness by the administrators trying to respond to citizen and public interest groups, (2) difficulties in representation and legitimacy, (3) the style and tactics of the participating groups, and (4) the lack of effective measures for evaluating citizen group proposals.[15] Administrators often respond quickly to the demands of citizen groups in order to demonstrate their responsiveness and to generate greater public support for their programs and agencies. However, the short-term benefits of such a response may lead to long-term problems, or the interests of a small vocal group may be satisfied to the detriment of the general public. Often the agency's less visible but equally necessary activities are lost in the shuffle as more popular activities and efforts to maintain good public relations receive the bulk of its attention and resources. The age-old problem of agencies' becoming dominated by clientele groups is also a worry to administrators. Some employees feel compelled to continue supporting their clientele's interests because of the group's influence over the agency.

Another difficulty is determining how representative such groups actually are. Groups tend to suggest that they have a much wider constituency than is actually the case, and many become very self-righteous in their approach. Agency personnel need to recognize that there are many perspectives and groups that must be considered. Although public interest groups, for example, portray themselves as serving no special interests, they normally are in fact devoted to some particular concern and are as likely as any other group is to perceive issues narrowly.

Another approach to humanizing and democratizing the public service favors advocacy administration. The idea here is to develop agents of change who will redirect the way public service carries out its mission.[16] Such a position is in contrast with the traditional approach to the merit system in which the public servant is to maintain a completely neutral stance on controversial issues and policymaking in general. Those who favor advocacy administration believe that public policy ignores many people and groups because only those who have power or know the rules of the game can really participate. The poor and others cannot hope to compete with well-organized and economically powerful interests. The solution is to introduce change agents into the bureaucracy whose function is to organize and mobilize those who are now outside the political process. The proponents of change agents in the public service have met with much resistance, to say the least, but they have made a contribution insofar as they have induced the public service to analyze itself and its role. Many agencies have created ombudsmen or clientele-citizen advocates to monitor the interests of clients or potential clients.

Summary

The public service in a democracy is usually considered to be the servant of the general public, and as such it should be responsive to that public. In recent years, efforts to make it responsive have included making the public service representative. Thus, equal employment opportunity and affirmative action programs try to make sure that all segments of society have the opportunity to compete for public jobs and, once employed, to be treated fairly in the personnel processes. Through affirmative action and equal employment opportunity, the public service can become more sensitive to all interests and thus accomplish the goal of being democratically responsive. An extension of the equal employment and affirmative action efforts is the concept of comparable worth. Currently a very visible issue, comparable worth is the equal pay for work of comparable value. Efforts are under way in many jurisdictions to institute comparable worth as policy in the public personnel system. Though proponents have been successful in some cases, there is also much resistance to the concept.

Other attempts at democratizing the public service include increasing the access of groups without political power to government agencies. Thus, advocacy adminstration and concerns with equity in service delivery try to make agencies and their personnel sensitive to the needs of their clientele and those who have few resources with which to participate in the political process.

NOTES

1. Frederick C. Mosher, *Democracy and the Public Service* (New York: Oxford University Press, 1968), pp. 11–13; and David H. Rosenbloom and Jeannette G. Featherstonhaugh, "Passive and Active Representation in the

Federal Service: A Comparison of Blacks and Whites," *Social Science Quarterly*, 57 (March 1977), 873–882.

2. For instance, see Rosenbloom and Featherstonhaugh; Lee Sigelman and Robert L. Carter, "Passive and Active Representation in the Federal Service: A Reanalysis," *Social Science Quarterly*, 58 (March 1978), 724–726; and Rosenbloom's and Featherstonhaugh's response, pp. 726–728 of the same issue.

3. David H. Rosenbloom and Douglas Kinnard, "Bureaucratic Representation and Bureaucratic Behavior: An Exploratory Analysis," *Midwest Review of Public Administration*, 11 (March 1977), 35–42.

4. Samuel Krislov and David H. Rosenbloom, *Representative Bureaucracy*, 2nd ed. (Englewood Cliffs, N.J.: Prentice-Hall, 1984); note this important consideration throughout the book. John Gardner, *Excellence: Can We Be Equal and Excellent Too?* (New York: Harper & Row, 1961), also bases much of his analysis on this point. Nathan Glazer discusses the negative implications of the issue in his *Affirmative Discrimination: Ethnic Inequality and Public Policy* (New York: Basic Books, 1975).

5. Thomas R. Dye, *The Politics of Equality* (Indianapolis: Bobbs-Merrill, 1971), provides an excellent history of the development of equal rights for blacks; pp. 230–235 deal specifically with how the control over institutions by Caucasians resulted in roadblocks for blacks. John Kenneth Galbraith, *Economics and the Public Purpose* (Boston: Houghton-Mifflin, 1973), chap. 23, explains the reasons for females' lack of access and suggests some strong action to remedy the situation, as does Helene Markoff, "The Federal Women's Program," *Public Administration Review*, 34 (January-February 1974), 18–29.

6. See Glazer, *Affirmative Discrimination;* and Sidney Hook, "On Discrimination: Part One," in Lucy W. Sells, ed., *Toward Affirmative Action: New Directions for Institutional Research* (San Francisco: Jossey-Bass, 1974). Also see Leonard B. Mandelbaum, "Affirmative Action Preference Systems: The Case for Human Resource Development," *Review of Public Personnel Administration*, 3 (Spring 1983), 1–14, for a good review of arguments for and against affirmative action.

7. Harry Kranz, *The Participatory Bureaucracy: Women and Minorities in a More Representative Public Service* (Lexington, Mass.: Lexington Books, 1976); David H. Rosenbloom, *Federal Equal Employment Opportunity: Politics and Public Personnel Administration* (New York: Praeger, 1977); N. Joseph Cayer and Lee Sigelman, "Minorities and Women in State and Local Government: 1973–75," *Public Adminstration Review* 40 (September-October 1980), 443–450; Patricia Huckle, "A Decade's Difference: Mid-Level Managers and Affirmative Action," *Public Personnel Management* 12 (Fall 1983), 249–257; and Nelson C. Dometrius and Lee Sigelman, "Assessing Progress Toward Affirmative Action Goals in State and Local Government: A New Benchmark," *Public Administration Review*, 44 (May-June 1984), 241–246.

8. Joy Ann Grune and Nancy Reder, "Pay Equity: An Innovative Public Policy Approach to Eliminating Sex-based Wage Discrimination," *Public Personnel Management*, 13 (Spring 1984), 70–80.

9. Elaine Johansen, *Comparable Worth: The Myth and the Movement*

(Boulder, Colo.: Westview Press, 1984), p. 14. Johansen's book presents the most thorough analysis available of the origins and development of comparable worth.

10. 454 U.S. 161 (1981).

11. H. George Frederickson, "Toward a New Public Administration," in Frank Marini, ed., *Toward a New Public Administration* (San Francisco: Chandler, 1971), chap. 11; and Machael Harmon, *Action Theory for Public Administration* (New York: Longman, 1981).

12. David K. Hart, "Social Equity, Justice, and the Equitable Administrator," *Public Administration Review*, 34 (January-February 1974), 3–11, has an excellent discussion of the definitional and conceptual problems.

13. As suggested throughout Frank Marini, ed., *Toward a New Public Administration*. Also see Hazel Henderson, "Information and the New Movements for Citizen Participation," *Annals of the American Academy of Political and Social Science*, 412 (March 1974) 34–43.

14. D. Stephen Cupps, "Emerging Problems of Citizen Participation," *Public Administration Review*, 37 (September-October), 478–487. Also see Derick W. Brinkerhoff, "Linking Accountability, Client Participation, and Quality of Life in the Public Sector: A Structural Framework," *Review of Public Personnel Administration*, 3 (Fall 1982), 67–76.

15. This discussion is based largely on Cupps, "Problems of Citizen Participation," which presents an excellent evaluation of citizen participation.

16. Marini, *Toward a New Public Administration*, is based on this position. For one of the best presentations of this position, see Louis C. Gawthrop, *Administrative Politics and Social Change* (New York: St. Martin's Press, 1971).

SUGGESTED READINGS

Davis, Charles E., and Jonathan P. West. "Implementing Public Programs: Equal Employment Opportunity, Affirmative Action, and Administrative Policy Options." *Review of Public Personnel Administration*, 4 (Summer 1984), 16–30.

Doherty, Mary Helen, and Ann Harriman. "Comparable Worth: The Equal Employment Issue of the 1980s." *Review of Public Personnel Administration*, 1 (Summer 1981), 11–31.

Frederickson, H. George, and Ralph Clark Chandler, eds. "Citizenship and Public Administration: Proceedings of the National Conference on Citizenship and Public Service." *Public Administration Review*, 44 (Special Issue, March 1984), 99–209.

Hendricks, Judith J. "The Prognosis for Affirmative Action at the State Level: A Study of Affirmative Action Implementation in Delaware." *Review of Public Personnel Administration*, 4 (Summer 1984), 57–70.

Hudson, William T., and Walter D. Broadnax. "Equal Opportunity As Public Policy." *Public Personnel Management*, 11 (Fall 1982), 268–276.

Johansen, Elaine. *Comparable Worth: The Myth and the Movement.* Boulder, Colo.: Westview Press, 1984.

———. "Managing the Revolution: The Case of Comparable Worth." *Review of Public Personnel Administration,* 4 (Spring 1984), 14–27.

Karnig, Albert K., Susan A. Welch, and Richard A. Eribes. "Employment of Women by Cities in the Southwest." *Social Science Journal,* 21 (Fall 1984), 41–48.

Lovrich, Nicholas P., Jr., and Brent S. Steel. "Affirmative Action and Productivity in Law Enforcement Agencies." *Review of Public Personnel Administration,* 4 (Fall 1983), 55–66.

Pearson, William M. "State Executives' Attitudes Toward a Democratic Ideology." *Midwest Review of Public Administration,* 11 (December 1977), 270–280.

Reichenberg, Neil E., ed. "Special Issue: Comparable Worth." *Public Personnel Management,* 12 (Winter 1983), 323–466.

Remick, Helen. "The Comparable Worth Controversy." *Public Personnel Management,* 10 (Winter 1981), 371–383.

Roberts, Robert N. " 'Last-Hired, First-Fired' and Public Employee Layoffs: The Equal Employment Opportunity Dilemma." *Review of Public Personnel Administration,* 2 (Fall 1981), 29–48.

Rosenbloom, David H. "The Declining Salience of Affirmative Action in Federal Personnel Management." *Review of Public Personnel Administration,* 4 (Summer 1984), 31–40.

Saltzstein, Grace Hall. "Personnel Directors and Female Employment Representation: A New Addition to Models of Equal Employment Opportunity Policy." *Social Science Quarterly,* 64 (December 1983), 734–746.

Smith, Russell L. "Representative Bureaucracy: A Research Note on Demographic Representation in State Bureaucracies." *Review of Public Personnel Administration,* 1 (Fall 1980), 1–13.

Thompson, Frank J. "Deregulation at the EEOC: Prospects and Implications." *Review of Public Personnel Administration,* 4 (Summer 1984), 41–56.

———. "Minority Groups in Public Bureaucracies: Are Passive and Active Representation Linked? *Administration and Society,* 8 (August 1976), 201–226.

Welch, Susan A., Albert K. Karnig, and Richard A. Eribes. "Changes in Hispanic Local Public Employment in the Southwest." *Western Political Quarterly,* 36 (December 1983), 660–673.

Wynia, Bob L. "Federal Bureaucrats' Attitudes Toward a Democratic Ideology." *Public Administration Review,* 34 (March-April 1974), 156–162.

Case 8.1: Nepotism

Carl Cey has been employed by the state Department of Health and Welfare for ten years as a case worker and case worker supervisor in the Welfare Division. He has been married to his wife Martha for fifteen years. Hilary Ruiz is the assistant director of the Health Division and has worked for the department for twelve years. Hilary is the wife of Martha's brother Esteban.

Carl has received excellent-to-outstanding performance evaluations during his employment with the department and was recently awarded a meritorious service honor by the state Civil Service System. Imagine his surprise, then, when he received a termination notice. The reason for his termination was violation of the state's nepotism policy which prohibits the hiring of immediate relatives in the same department. But the termination notice stipulates that it will be rescinded if Carl files for divorce from Martha within thirty days. Being happily married, Carl has no intention of filing for divorce.

Appeals within the department and Civil Service System have proved unfruitful for Carl, even though his employers knew of his relationship to Hilary from the day he was employed. Thus, he is now filing suit against the department and the state to retain his position.

INSTRUCTIONS:

1. Assume the role of Carl's attorney. What are the bases on which the case might be pursued?
2. Assume the role of the attorney for the state and department. How might she defend the policy and termination?
3. As a consultant to the state Civil Service System, what would you recommend to avoid such a suit in the future?

Case 8.2: The Affirmative Action Plan

You have been hired as the director of the affirmative action office for the city of Harmony. The city has never had an affirmative action plan before, and you have the task of drawing one up as your first priority. As you might imagine, there are many conflicts over specific policy recommendations. Your job is to come up with policies that comply with the law but also consider the interests of various parties in the personnel system.

One of the thorniest issues is a policy regarding how to handle layoffs during periods of retrenchment. You are faced by strong public employee unions that insist that layoffs be based on reverse seniority or last hired, first fired. You also hear from minority employees who have their group of Employees United for Personnel Justice (EUPJ) and female employees who have organized the Women's Networking Alliance (WNA). The EUPJ and WNA both are petitioning you to protect minority and female employees who were hired to support the equal employment opportunity objectives of the city's personnel policy.

INSTRUCTIONS:

Draft a layoff or reduction-in-force policy statement for the affirmative action plan, and justify the provisions of your policy statement.

9

The Challenges of Public Personnel

P ublic personnel management has been presented in this book as an amalgam of processes, institutions, and policies shaped by various forces in its environment. Like other activities in our political system, public personnel administration is always changing. Because change in our system is incremental and gradual, the field is a product of constant adjustment to changing technology, citizen and political demands, and changes in managers and employees. Experts do not agree on what the future is likely to bring in personnel management, but there seems to be a general consensus on some of the forces that are likely to affect the field.

Technological Change

It is impossible to predict what sort of technological advances will develop, but it is certain that there will be advances and that public personnel management will be affected by them. With new technology come new expertise and ways of solving old problems. The introduction of the computer after World War II has been accentuated in recent years by the advent of the minicomputer and the personal computer. Because of computers, personnel offices have been able to operate more efficiently, and at the same time, personnel functions have changed. Concerns about the physical effects of computers' video components and alienation associated with working with machines rather than other people are just a couple of the newer problems faced by personnel systems. Counseling and monitoring are helping resolve them.

As new technology is introduced to all types of work, the personnel offices must also cope with the obsolete skills of their existing employees. Training programs, reassignment, and the like are being used to deal with such problems. The ability of advanced technology to improve productivity is always dear to the hearts of managers, but it may also have negative effects, such as the employees' anxiety and deteriorating morale.

New technology often brings with it new professional associations, which can have both negative and positive effects for the personnel system. On the positive side, professional associations often establish standards of behavior for their members, thus providing peer pressure to use the technology with integrity. Professional associations, however, may also temper individuals' loyalty to their employing organization. Their loyalty to the profession often precedes that to their employer, and so their commitment to the organization is affected. Too, professional associations may develop acceptable qualifications for given jobs or dictate which professionals can do what particular work. This may also conflict with the work organization.

Expertise carries with it political power as well. Professional expertise often affects political decision making, and the experts may challenge the power of the legislative and elected executive officers. Because elected public officials usually are in office for a limited time, they often defer to professional experts. Legislative bodies, in particular, are often alarmed by the need to rely on experts, because it usually means that more power flows to the executive branch, as that is where the permanent cadre of experts resides.

Citizen–Taxpayer Concerns

The political environment of the 1980s is forcing public personnel administration to work with limited resources. The national election of 1984 seemed to reaffirm that the people want limited government and are not in a mood to give blank checks to governmental jurisdictions. As a result, personnel administrators face the challenge of stretching their limited resources to buy even more than they did in the past. And because government is affected by inflation like everyone else, the task is not an easy one.

Productivity improvement efforts will continue to be among the top priorities of public managers as they attempt to deal with limited resources. Collective bargaining efforts are especially likely to be affected by these problems. Agreements on greater pay and benefits are likely to be increasingly tied to the employees' greater productivity. Cooperative programs among jurisdictions are also likely to continue to expand as a way of limiting costs. Such arrangements for recruiting, examining, and certifying are certain to attract more attention in the future. For small jurisdictions, these programs can help improve their ability to perform personnel functions without adding greatly to their costs. Though the initial benefit to the larger jurisdictions may not be as apparent, they will be able to save resources by sharing the costs of such operations with other units of government using the services.

Contracting out for services may also help jurisdictions satisfy demands for less costly government service. Smaller jurisdictions often find that large capital investments are needed to offer many services and that they can contract, at a smaller price, with private firms or other jurisdictions for the services. Some cities, for example, have found that they can contract with private water companies or fire protection services more cheaply than they can provide the services on their own. Contracting with other jurisdictions for water, health, and computer services is also common among local governments. Not the least of the savings is in benefits. Governmental jurisdictions find that they can avoid costly retirement programs and the like by contracting out rather than employing their own people to provide the service.

Personnel managers are affected by the contracting-out process in that they often are responsible for certifying that such services can be contracted. They also may be required to monitor the personnel aspects of the contracting process. Thus, they may have to oversee policies relating to nondiscrimination and other rules and regulations related to personnel. Contracting for services is particularly popular in the current political climate, as it brings government closer to the private sector model.

The image of the public service is a constant problem for public personnel managers. Public managers must realize that much of the general public looks down on public employees. Such a view hampers recruitment efforts and the legitimacy of public programs. To overcome this, efforts to ensure public employees' ethical behavior will likely continue to be a major issue in the near future.

Equity and Interest Group Demands

Equal employment opportunity and affirmative action were among the most significant personnel issues of the 1970s. They are still important but they have been deemphasized somewhat, largely because of the current administration's decision not to enforce those policies vigorously. Consequently, all levels of government feel under less pressure to follow these policies in their personnel activities. Nonetheless, affected groups, especially women and minorities, are likely to keep up the pressure. With help from the courts and from some political leaders, the issues are likely to remain important through the 1980s. More and more attention is being focused on the quality of employment of target groups. Quality is measured by the level of position held and the pay attached to that position. Whereas attention in the 1970s tended to go to opening the doors to being hired in the first place, the current concerns are with promotional ladders and success in moving up the hierarchy.

Perhaps the coming years' most controversial demands are those being made by homosexual groups. Although a few states and localities have extended employment protection to gays, it is still an emotional issue. The intensity of these reactions to gay rights can create many problems for personnel managers. The extent of the emotionalism is illustrated by the recent demands of at least one straight police officer in San Francisco. He did not want a homosexual officer viewing his body and so insisted on separate dressing facilities when the department began recruiting gays. Although this complaint is rather trifling, it demonstrates the strength of feelings involved. Public personnel systems are likely to continue to be a focal point for gays as they press their case for nondiscrimination. And as they demonstrate their political power, as they have in some jurisdictions, they will achieve results just as other groups have.

Comparable worth is the newest issue in making public personnel management more equitable. Many people are calling it the issue of the 1980s, and the attention paid it in the courts and in legislative bodies as well as union halls makes it certain to continue to challenge public personnel administrators.

Employee Demands

Another facet of equity will be demands to protect the rights of employees. As our society continues to become more complex and impersonal, legal and institutional means will be used to maintain human dignity in the personnel process. One effect may be stricter rules and regulations governing the managers' control over employees, thus weakening management's position. It is likely that managers and supervisors will become more aware of needing to deal with people as individuals. The rights of employees in the appeals and grievance processes will probably lead to more training of supervisory personnel in labor relations.

Participation by employees in the decisions affecting them will continue to be a high priority for them and their organizations. The well-established trend toward collective bargaining has provided a strong mechanism for employee input into decisions. Many employers will accommodate their employees' demands to avoid further collective bargaining, but many also will use the bargaining process. Collective bargaining is currently under attack by many political leaders and managers, but it is here to stay, though its form is likely to change. In the current political environment, labor organizations find it difficult to take a militant stance; thus, they are looking for other ways of working within the system to have their concerns considered. For the short run at least, less militant and more cooperative approaches are likely to prevail. However, if the economy improves and unemployment drops greatly, labor will be in a stronger position once again, and militance may return.

Employees' participation goes beyond their jobs. In our society, in which everyone demands a right to be heard, public employees will maintain their pressure to be given their rights as citizens in a democracy. Assaults on the Hatch Act and on other restrictions against public employees will continue, and the right to dissent will be claimed ever more strongly. For the personnel system, if such changes occur, it will mean more difficulty in maintaining the balance between political responsiveness and the neutrality of the public service.

Litigation

Taking issues to court seems to be the way to resolve all problems in our society, and personnel managers constantly find themselves the objects of litigation. Equal employment opportunity and comparable worth have spawned a lot of litigation, but other issues have come up as well. Challenges to every aspect of personnel management are common and are not likely to abate. The increasing number of lawsuits necessitates new expertise in the personnel field. Personnel managers have not been noted for their legal training, and legal staffs have not been particularly well trained in the public personnel field. That situation is currently changing, as personnel offices need people to represent them in all aspects of employee relations.

Summary

Many forces will change the field of public personnel management. The same changes that affect the rest of society will be important to managers of public personnel. But what will not change is that public personnel management is a product of the political environment in which it operates.

SUGGESTED READINGS

Beckman, Norman, and James P. Hellings. "A Public Personnel Policy to Help Management in the 1980s." *Review of Public Personnel Administration*, 1 (Spring 1981), 53–69.
"Crucial Issues for Public Personnel Professionals." *Public Personnel Management*, 13 (Special Issue, Spring 1984), 1–69.

Index